# 20 Steps to Better Management

## John McBride & Nick Clark

*Learning Resources*

## BBC Books

# About the authors

**B**oth John McBride and Nick Clark work for the business psychology consultancy Nicholson McBride. The company has worked with over 100 organizations, in most industry sectors, and specializes in the design and implementation of transformation programmes which bring out the best in people.

As the Managing Director of Nicholson McBride, John works with clients to help them improve business performance, including changing organizational culture, improving communications, developing teams, and helping managers align their personal skills with the requirements of the businesses they lead.

Having worked in the advertising industry and as a freelance scriptwriter, Nick completed an MSc in occupational psychology at the University of London and joined Nicholson McBride as a Consultant. His work involves developing management competencies, enhancing team performance, and helping managers cope with change.

# Acknowledgements

The authors would like to thank John Nicholson for his inspiration, input and guiding influence. Other Nicholson McBride consultants who have contributed their ideas, expertize and (most importantly) enthusiasm include Jane Clarke, Helen Fisher, Laura Nichols, Charles Sutton, Sarah Sweetman, Cathy Walton and Jordan Whitten. Thanks also to Fiona Thompson for her contribution, to Central Services – EJ, Sal, Max, and Helen – for their vital support work, and to Sebastian Bailey for researching the booklist.

For his patience and dedication as copy editor, particular thanks are due to Peter Milson, and within BBC Books, the authors would like to thank Charlotte Lochhead for flexibility in the face of adversity, and Nicky Copeland for commissioning the book and providing constructive feedback throughout the process.

We would also like to acknowledge the valuable contribution made by the BBC production team, namely producer Robert Cooke, associate producer Michelle Jones and executive producer Mike Flood Page.

Finally, thanks must especially go to our families and friends for their input and backup. In particular, this book is dedicated to Eileen, Fiona, and Kate; and to Becky, Bailey, and Rudkin.

This book is published to accompany the BBC television series entitled
*20 Steps to Better Management* which was first broadcast in 1996.
Executive Producer Mike Flood Page
Producer Robert Cooke

Published by BBC Books,
an imprint of BBC Worldwide Publishing,
BBC Worldwide Limited, Woodlands,
80 Wood Lane, London W12 0TT

First published 1996
© Nicholson McBride 1996
The moral right of the authors has been asserted

ISBN 0 563 38772 6

Designed by Harry Green

Set in Palatino and Futura
Printed in Great Britain by Martins of Berwick Ltd,
Berwick-upon-Tweed.
Bound in Great Britain by Hunter & Foulis Ltd, Edinburgh
Cover printed by Clays Ltd, St Ives plc

# Contents

# Introduction

The modern world of work – unremitting change, colliding priorities, pressure for results. No business or part of a business is immune. The modern manager must reduce costs, stay in touch with technological developments and understand the dynamics of rapidly changing marketplaces and customer demand. The job has never been more exacting.

Whether you succeed or fail is inextricably linked with how your people perform. The temptation may be to retreat to the apparent safety of the bunker and issue orders. But managers can't rely on authority and coercion any more. To succeed, organizations have to be flexible and responsive, with decision-making devolved all the way down to the front line.

So *involvement* is the watchword. Managers must motivate people, inspiring commitment and action and encouraging creativity. They must harness the experience, energies and skills of diverse groups of people and build first-class teams to resolve problems, identify opportunities and make sense of the huge volume of information now available.

These are tough challenges. How well do you think you're meeting them? For example, are you really helping others to achieve? How good are you at giving feedback? How confident are you that you can resolve conflict in your team? Are you getting your message across clearly? Are you accomplished in the art of influence?

This book aims to help you build or hone your management skills so that you can provide people with the support and opportunities they need to thrive, enabling them to relate personal and team achievement to the success of an organization – and so experience that success as if it were their own.

# 1 Making the most of yourself

**Could this be you?** My new position is a move in the right direction. I'm grateful for the change. People here know of me, but few have worked directly with me before, so I can start with a clean slate. And I think perhaps I need to! Towards the end of my last job, I had one or two unpleasant surprises. I've always thought of myself as a modern manager – I try to take a balanced view; I'm open to change; I consult and involve people; my door's always open. Sadly, though, this wasn't how everyone saw it. In an appraisal I was criticized for being passive and indecisive. Obviously I need to find a new way of doing things, so that I come across more effectively. But where do I start?

The first rule of management must be: 'Know yourself'. If you want to improve your own performance and that of others, it's vital to be honest with yourself about your strengths and your weaknesses. This chapter looks at how boosting your self-awareness can be a springboard for positive change, and in particular at how to improve your assertiveness and self-confidence.

## Challenging your assumptions

First of all, it's important to challenge the following common assumptions, each of which can create false expectations and prevent you becoming an effective manager. See if you recognize any of them.

*I must perform perfectly, always and in all respects.*
No one is perfect at anything all the time, let alone at everything. Accepting that you have weaknesses is vital if you are to improve your own performance. You will, however, also have certain attributes you can be proud of, as well as things that you do better than most people. It may be worth listing them, fighting the false modesty that is so often an obstacle to self-esteem.

*Everyone must like me and approve of everything I do.*
Accepting that you cannot please all the people all the time is one of the most important lessons you need to learn. For one thing, different people have different interests. Any decision is bound to displease someone, which is why people suffering from this assumption find decision-making so painful.

Moreover, just as you may make unrealistic demands on others, so other people sometimes look for assistance you may be unable or unwilling to provide. For example, someone in your team may benefit from a style of management that is alien to you. But even if you can't meet their expectations, you can usually lessen their disappointment by explaining why you are unable to oblige, and the benefits of your preferred style.

This assumption that you should try to keep everyone happy can trigger two other damaging assumptions: that there's something dreadfully wrong with *you*, or that everything is someone else's fault. You need to boost your self-confidence to the point at which the loss of one person's approval is of no real consequence (see page 17, 'Improving your self-confidence').

*I have a right to expect other people to give me everything I want.*
Not only do you have no right to expect this, but this assumption is the antithesis of the way an effective manager's mind works. Experience teaches us that we never get everything we want from other people: there are many times when other people can't – and probably shouldn't – give us what we ask them for.

People who don't give you what you want may have an excellent reason for it – they have their own lives, their own pressures, and their own deadlines and concerns. It's very unlikely that they're acting out of spite or bloody-mindedness.

*I am the product and the victim of my personal history.*
Of course your past affects who you are today but you don't have to be stuck with it.

People develop and change spontaneously and it's open to anyone to seek to speed up or shape the process. To some extent we have to work to scripts that have been written for us, but this doesn't mean we must passively accept these scripts and live them out. We have the power to rewrite them.

*If I am unhappy, it's someone else's fault.*
Blaming other people for your dissatisfaction gives you an excuse not to

make an effort to put things right. By projecting your feelings on to others and wasting your energy devising schemes to avenge imagined wrongs, you are simply postponing the hunt for solutions. Attributing blame is futile and irrelevant when there's a job to be done.

## Developing self-knowledge

In order to manage others successfully, you need to understand both what sort of person you are and how others see you. If you don't, your motives are likely to be misinterpreted and your messages misunderstood.

Some people have no guile, no secret selves – what you see is what they are. Others have public and private selves. Do you want to be a different person in public and in private – a slob at home and a well-dressed executive at work? There is no right and wrong answer to this question, but either way you need to be alert to other people's perceptions of you.

## Understanding how others see you

Even very open people don't behave predictably in all situations. Other people have to interpret what you do, and can only guess at what's going on in your mind.

So as a manager you need to be aware of possible different interpretations of your behaviour. What you regard as flexibility, for example, others may see as inconsistency.

Here is a list of other possible misunderstandings, in which well-intentioned behaviour is subject to a much less charitable interpretation.

| How you see yourself | How others may see you |
|---|---|
| confident | arrogant |
| enterprising | exploitative |
| humorous | frivolous |
| ambitious | ruthless |
| helpful | controlling |
| forceful | bullying |
| competitive | combative |
| open to change | wishy-washy |
| thorough | obsessive |
| tolerant | indifferent |
| focused | tunnel-visioned |
| supportive | interfering |
| generous | irresponsible |

Don't be a slave to other people's perceptions of you, but do try to understand and appreciate them. Keep your eyes and ears open to the possibility of misinterpretation. You might, for example, begin to suspect there is a problem if legitimate requests are not complied with, or people react in unexpected ways. People you thought were allies might become inexplicably cool or wary. You might start hearing rumours. On the other hand, colleagues might simply tell you plainly what they think!

To try to keep misunderstandings to a minimum, you should always be as explicit as you can (see chapter 11, page 86, 'Communicating clearly'). Test that people have understood what you want and what you're saying by asking them to put it in their own words, or by using expressions such as 'I'm not sure I've made myself clear...'. Seek constant feedback about how you come across and listen carefully to what people say (see page 26, 'Active Listening').

You can actively encourage feedback by informally inviting comments or by getting colleagues to take part in a simple exercise. Ask them (anonymously!) to list what they think are your strengths and weaknesses in terms of your personal style and the way in which you interact with others. You could also ask them to list what that they think you could improve immediately if you put your mind to it, and what you might be able to improve in the longer term. You could even design a simple form for your colleagues to fill in.

Meanwhile, being as honest as you can, go through the same process yourself: write down your strengths and weaknesses, what you think can be changed immediately and your long-term aims. Comparing your own assessment with that of others may bring a few unpleasant surprises, but there will be a much higher price to pay if you don't try to address discrepancies.

## Getting ready for change

Most of us have only fulfilled a fraction of our potential. It is this that makes the desire for self-improvement and real change more than just wishful thinking.

Don't be taken in by those who say that some people can't change or that there is something unnatural about trying. We *can* change, provided we choose the right things to work on and set about it realistically.

It is very difficult, if not impossible, to change major personality characteristics. However, most people only want to change aspects of their behaviour or the feelings they have about them. For example, a very shy person could live with their shyness if it did not make them clam up when confronted by a stranger. This behavioural change is one it is quite possible to make. Similarly, you can increase your assertiveness (see page 13) and your ability to get on with other people – provided you really have the will to change and plan matters sensibly.

Before you begin, you need to establish whether it is really you that you want to change, or some aspect of your life-style or working circumstances. Before starting to round the corners off a square peg, make sure that it wouldn't be better just to find – or try to make – a square hole!

Here are some principles that will help you prepare for change:

- Once again, know yourself! We all have different needs and it's up to each of us to know what they are, and to try to avoid getting into a situation in which we are just pandering to someone else's wishes, or trying to do a job according to guidelines designed with someone else in mind. You must establish how you work most effectively and try to create a work-style to match – provided of course it's not in complete conflict with those around you. Be prepared to educate others in your way of doing things.
- Don't be your own worst enemy! It's possible that partners, colleagues and friends will feel threatened by your changing, but the biggest enemy to change has to be your own attitude.
- Don't underestimate yourself or your capacity to change – and don't passively accept other people's estimation of you.
- Take your shortcomings seriously but don't make totally unrealistic demands on yourself.

## The three stages of personal change

Change is a three-stage operation.

The first stage consists of imagining what you will be like when you have changed. If you want to overcome shyness, for example, you should imagine yourself behaving in a more confident and extrovert manner in specific situations such as team meetings.

In the second stage, you should behave as if you were already the person you'd like to be, acting out the part you have imagined, so that you get the feel of what it would feel like to be such a person.

The third stage of change is when this role-playing becomes reality. Often this is a gradual process, a matter of losing self-consciousness and no longer asking whether the person refusing a cigarette or insisting on their rights can really be you.

## Checklist for change

Here is a checklist of the steps that can make change a reality:

- Commit yourself to the idea that change is possible.
- Ask yourself how well you know yourself and understand your true motives. Explore your reasons for wanting to change.
- Decide exactly what it is that needs to be changed. Is it you or just some aspect of your lifestyle?
- Make sure you understand and are prepared for the likely consequences of change.
- Make sure the change is something you can start on right now. The *mañana* spirit is fatal to successful change.
- If you want to make major changes, set yourself a series of modest, short-term goals rather than going for the jackpot from the beginning.
- Imagine how you would be if you had made a particular change, and try to act out the part.
- Avoid negative thinking. Don't talk yourself into failure, and don't allow yourself to be discouraged by other people's responses. Don't make too much of temporary setbacks.
- Keep a constant check on how well you are doing. Reward yourself for successes, either by allowing yourself an indulgence, or, preferably, by simple self-congratulation. If you can, get other people who are sympathetic to what you are doing to help.

The following sections look at two specific aspects of personality and behaviour that people commonly want to change – both of which are crucial if you want to be an effective manager.

## Assertiveness

Assertiveness involves expressing yourself honestly while respecting the feelings of others. The more assertive your behaviour becomes, the more likely you are to know who you are and what you want – from your colleagues and from the job itself.

To test your assertiveness, ask yourself the following questions:

|  | Yes | No |
|---|---|---|
| 1 Do you find it difficult to say no to any kind of demand made on you? |  |  |
| 2 If someone jumped to the front of a queue, would you do something about it? |  |  |
| 3 Do you usually put yourself second in family matters? |  |  |

|  | Yes | No |
|---|---|---|

4 Do you believe that it is necessary to fight for your rights, and that if you don't you risk losing them altogether?

5 Do you make a point of complaining if you are sold shoddy goods?

6 Do you have great difficulty in leaving situations when you have had enough?

7 Do you find it difficult to get rid of a sales rep who is persistent and wasting your time?

8 Do you hesitate about asking a stranger directions in the street?

9 If you were working on a committee, would you tend to take charge of things?

10 If you have been given poor service in a restaurant or hotel, do you always make a fuss?

For questions 2, 4, 5, 9 and 10, score 2 points for each 'yes' answer, and zero for every 'No'. For questions 1, 3, 6, 7 and 8, score 2 points for each 'no' and zero for each 'yes'.

The higher your score, the more assertive you are. A score of 14 or more suggests that you have what is sometimes called a 'strong' personality. You insist that other people respect your rights, and you may even be seen as 'pushy'. A score of 8 or less, on the other hand, indicates that you are submissive, a follower rather than a leader, and that people are likely to take advantage of you.

Assertive people strike a balance between undue aggression and passivity. Think of a situation when a colleague asked you to stay and work late when you had planned to go out.

A passive person might say something like: 'Er, I'm sorry, I don't know. I was thinking of going out... But if it's really important, I suppose I could see the play another time.'

An aggressive person might reply: 'You must be joking. You can't manage your workload, so you expect me to be a mug and help you out? Forget it.'

An *assertive* person, in contrast, would be relaxed and controlled, using non-judgmental language to put his or her point across, saying, for example: 'Sorry, I can't help you tonight. I've got something else planned.'

Whereas aggression involves trying to deprive others of their rights,

assertiveness means standing up for your legitimate rights. Assertive people:
- are direct and honest
- respect themselves and others
- know and can articulate their rights
- recognize their own needs
- take responsibility for their own actions
- don't take rejection personally
- don't avoid confrontation

There are a whole range of assertiveness tactics that you can use to your advantage when people try to make you feel guilty, coerce you into doing something, or criticize you unfairly. Here are some of the most effective.

### CUTTING TO THE CORE MESSAGE

A person who's afraid to say what they feel will often pad out their sentences with ums and ers and phrases such as: 'Sorry to interrupt you...'; 'I can see you're busy, but...'; 'If you see what I mean...'; 'You'll probably think this is stupid...' and so on. If you strip out the padding, your message will seem much more powerful and direct. Just compare these two different approaches:

'I'm sorry to bother you – you're obviously busy. But you see I really do need to use this office for a meeting. Would you mind terribly? If it's inconvenient, I could use the one next door.'

'I need this office for a meeting now. Could you move into the one next door, please?'

### PERSISTENCE

If you come across bullying tactics, you may need to change your normal way of operating. Repetition is one technique that works in this context. Once you have decided on your core message, try repeating it while remaining calm and keeping your voice at the same pitch. When the other person has heard you repeat 'I can't finish that project over the weekend' four times, it should finally sink in.

### KNOWING YOUR TRIGGERS

Once again, self-knowledge is crucial. You need to be aware of your 'triggers' – the types of criticism that really get to you. For example, you might see yourself as a bad time-keeper, or be sensitive about certain aspects of your physical appearance. If you are aware of these particular sensitivities, you will be less likely to react in an emotional way, and more able to distinguish whether or not the criticism is valid. That will help you deal with criticism more assertively.

## STICKING TO THE FACTS

If you're being criticized, you may be able to agree with the facts without agreeing with the criticism or reacting defensively or angrily. This tends to disarm someone if they are trying to manipulate or unnerve you. For example, if your boss says, 'You still haven't done that report due on Thursday, have you?', you could simply reply, 'No, I haven't.' This would nonplus someone who was expecting a denial or embarrassment, giving you time to follow up with a calm explanation.

## ACTIVE LISTENING

This means showing another person that you appreciate their position, and then reiterating your own. For example, someone might say, 'I hate the way you presented the latest sales figures. You made my department look like a failure.' Your reply should show that you have listened to what the other person is saying, and also state your own view of events. You might say, for instance, 'I'm sorry you didn't like the way I presented the sales figures, but the directors asked for them in that format.' (See also chapter 3, page 26, 'Active listening'.)

## AVOIDING ACCUSATION

When you are the person who has to criticize someone else or give negative feedback, it is important to focus on specific behaviour rather than personalities. It's also useful to concentrate on your own response, without directly attributing blame, for example saying 'I'm really worried about that' rather than 'You've really got me worried about that'. (See also page 68, 'Telling people what you think of them'.)

## BODY LANGUAGE

Body language also plays an important role in assertiveness. It's important to be physically at the same level as the person you're talking to – i.e. both sitting down or both standing up. You need to face the other person, but not so directly that they feel you are squaring up for a fight – it's better to stand or sit at a slight angle. Avoid nervous gestures such as touching the face, moving about too much or folding your arms across your chest.

# Improving your self-confidence

Self-confidence is closely related to assertiveness, and training yourself to act more assertively will help to boost your self-confidence. The following steps should also help:

- Make sure you measure what you achieve. Keep a success diary and look for things you can feel good about.
- Make a list of all your positive qualities. Don't be modest!
- Be aware of what and who makes you feel good about yourself and make sure you expose yourself to these influences at least as much as you expose yourself to negative ones.
- Don't look for examples to illustrate negative thoughts you have about yourself.
- Try to understand the pattern of your negative thoughts and look for ways of counteracting them.
- Seek feedback from others – people are often their own worst enemies, assuming others have negative views about them, when in fact they don't.

---

To sum up: if you want to make the most of yourself, first of all you'll need to identify exactly what you want to change. To do this you need to be honest with yourself about your assumptions, about the sort of person you are, and about your strengths and weaknesses. And you need to be aware of how others see you.

If you then set about making changes in a positive and realistic way, with the help of the guidelines given above, you should soon find that you hardly recognize the new, dynamic, assertive you!

---

# 2 You can't do it alone

**Could this be you?** I finally landed a team leader's job 18 months ago. I now have a couple of dozen people relying on me, so it's more important than ever that I'm the most up-to-date person in the outfit.

Recently I've had to get more involved in hands-on development work, as there's a blanket ban on recruitment and work keeps piling up. I'm working longer hours, and have had to make more time by cutting back on team meetings. In the last few weeks, there have been some worrying developments, though. A potentially good deal with a supplier fell through, and an exciting project I'd assumed was coming to my team has gone elsewhere. There have been mutterings that I should have gone to a couple of meetings, but more important things came up.

I know I can't do everything, and will have to rely on other people more. But when I know I'm the best person for a job it's hard to let someone else take over.

**M**any managers suffer from the delusion that they should have hands-on control of every aspect of their business. But the fact is that most businesses today are too complex, wide-ranging and fast-moving for one manager to be actively involved in every day-to-day decision.

As a result, managers with unrealistic expectations about what they can handle are likely to wind up feeling anxious and insecure. In an effort to master the situation they may attempt to tighten control still further, introducing more systems and procedures, losing perspective of their management role and becoming increasingly bogged down in detail.

This chapter looks at how you can avoid this by delegating effectively and building more productive working relationships within your team.

# The art of delegation

The first challenge is to acknowledge that you can't do everything yourself. Resources are available to help you meet your objectives, and the most important of these is the people you work with.

Once you've accepted that members of your team want to improve and can perform in extraordinary ways, your next step is to provide them with opportunities to grow and develop experience – i.e. to delegate to them.

Literally, delegation means using someone as a representative. Doing it effectively will bring a number of benefits:

- Top performers who seek out and enjoy challenges will be attracted to your team, and poor performers who don't want to be challenged will be deterred.
- Work won't come to a halt when you're out of the office.
- You'll have more time for forward-looking, strategic tasks such as developing teamwork, improving service, raising the quality of products and updating systems.
- Team members who have some responsibility, so they feel they will be praised for good results as well as constructively criticized for mistakes, are more likely to want to take on tasks.
- Personal and professional satisfaction is increased for all concerned
- You'll be using your budget more efficiently: it costs less if a member of your team performs a task, as their time is less expensive than yours.

All in all, everybody wins from effective delegation: team members have more opportunity to cultivate their careers and contribute to the firm; you free up your time for more productive work; and the business benefits from increased efficiency and staff satisfaction, and from a more dynamic environment.

Your team is more likely to fail through your doubting their abilities than through their inexperience – so what reasons do you find to resist delegation?

## Excuses for resisting the challenge

Here are some possible excuses for not delegating, all of which you must reject:

*In the time it takes to explain, I can do it myself* – in the short-term this may be true, but in the long term delegation will save you time.

*My team isn't yet capable* – they never will be unless you start incorporating delegation into their development plans.

*No one is up to it except me* – even if this is true, are you being too much of a perfectionist? Does the task need such a degree of excellence? If not, maybe someone else could do the job adequately in less time.

*I enjoy these tasks – losing them would make my job less interesting* – in the longer term, the improvement in staff morale and performance brought about by delegating will make your job easier and just as enjoyable.

## Traps to avoid

Simply delegating is not enough – the way you do it has a huge impact. Make sure you don't fall into any of the categories below:

### THE DUMPER

Off-loading only work you don't want to do is the least effective way of developing and motivating people. Your team will feel frustrated, resentful, overloaded and unable to plan their own work effectively. They will lack any sense of worth, achievement or personal development. You must delegate interesting and challenging projects as well.

### THE CONTROLLER

Lack of trust and an unwillingness to let go whatever the situation will waste much time and potential. Your people's growth will be restricted by your own narrow definition of their personal development.

### THE ABDICATOR

Simply abdicating responsibility and leaving people to sink or swim will make people feel insecure, unsupported and isolated. Even if they don't go under, they'll have to learn the hard way, and will probably make many mistakes along the way.

## Four levels of delegation

Different situations require different balances of control and delegation. The following should help you decide which is appropriate.

### I'LL DECIDE

This level involves delegating tasks but not responsibility. You hope the other person will follow your directions willingly, but if they feel unhappy about them, they will still be required to carry them out.

This approach is best with new members of a team who are enthusiastic and eager to learn, but who have limited knowledge and experience. They expect to be told what to do, and both need and accept close supervision. It's appropriate when you want to involve someone, but the job is too sensitive or important for you to relax your control. An example might be seeking a newcomer's help with a presentation of departmental results to the directors.

With this approach, it's vital to give clear messages and leave team members in no doubt as to whether they are responding to an order, a request or a suggestion. The danger in doing this is that it might impede someone's development by diminishing their role and increasing their dependence on you.

## WE'LL DISCUSS; I'LL DECIDE

At this level of delegation, control is diminishing, and coaching is the principal theme of supervision.

When in this mode, you may be able to accept every suggestion given by a colleague. When this is not possible, you should explain why an alternative would be more successful and then help him or her to learn the skills necessary to implement it. Team members must be made aware that all final decisions will be made by you.

This style is best when you want and value someone's input, but must retain ultimate responsibility, for example when recruiting new team members.

When using this approach, beware of deceiving your people by pretending to have a discussion when you've already decided exactly what will be done. If you do this you will forfeit their trust.

## WE'LL DISCUSS; WE'LL DECIDE

At this level, you and your colleague are aiming to agree solutions to problems or ways of handling projects.

This is appropriate when your colleague's understanding and skills in the area under consideration are roughly equal to your own, and you are both happy to share your knowledge and enthusiasm, for example when writing a marketing brief for a supplier.

When using this approach, beware of pretending to offer freedom when you're actually intending to maintain strict controls.

## WE'LL DISCUSS; YOU DECIDE

At this level, your colleague takes responsibility for the final decision after receiving input from you – for example deciding which of a number of candidates to recruit. This approach is best when you have insights or information to offer, but your colleague needs to assume responsibility because he or she will be affected by the consequences .

## YOU DECIDE; IF YOU NEED HELP, ASK

At this level you largely hand over control, whilst retaining ultimate authority and responsibility (see also chapter 16, page 117, 'Letting go'). Your role becomes that of a consultant, who makes suggestions, provides information, obtains resources and gives support if and when required. However, you will still need to define parameters carefully, leaving no possibility of misunderstanding.

This approach is best when colleagues can accept the challenges and disciplines of full delegation and work autonomously. They must both want and be equipped to achieve the highest possible performance standards. This sort of delegation is also particularly appropriate when the issues are personally important to your colleague.

There are two main dangers here. Firstly, though you're losing control, you're still responsible, so you must be confident in your colleague's ability to deliver. In addition you need to beware of overloading colleagues who aren't ready to take on the responsibility.

Remember, none of these approaches is inherently better than another. Each works well provided they are appropriate for the situation and parameters are well understood by you and members of your team.

## How to delegate

The first step is to make a shopping list of the things you do, and ask yourself the following questions:

- How much time do things take and how many tasks really *have* to be done by you?
- Which tasks don't you delegate because you like them? Should you be delegating any of these?
- Which tasks do you delegate because you hate them? Are there any you should be doing yourself?

Once you've decided what to delegate, the next steps are to:

- Select someone for the task. The person you choose will not necessarily be the one with the best skills or the most time available. You may want to encourage someone to develop their skills in areas in which they are weak. Also, what someone lacks in experience and skill, they may more than make up for in potential and motivation.
- Set a clear objective for the task. This should build confidence, develop and stretch (but beware of overloading or off-loading).
- Discuss the assignment and how the task fits into the big picture – why it's important for the organization.
- Explain why you've chosen the person for the task – that you value them and aren't just pushing unwanted work their way.

- Check for understanding and ask for comments.
- Make a delegation 'contract' establishing division of responsibility, resources available, how often you will follow up and how performance will be measured.
- Establish controls – budget, deadlines and when and how a formal review will take place.
- Make yourself available, particularly at critical times.
- Publicize the fact that the task has been delegated – the recognition of colleagues is a motivating factor.
- Evaluate the finished project. Concentrate on what went right (give praise for a job done well), and what went wrong (identify lessons learned not only for the person but for yourself too!).

## Building relationships

Delegating effectively is just one of the ways of building a relationship with your team. There are a number of reasons why good working relationships with team members are vital.

Firstly, they help you get more out of your team, as people will go the extra mile for those they trust and respect.

Secondly, being on good terms with your team helps ensure a flow of accurate information through both formal and informal channels. You need up-to-date intelligence on diverse areas to do your job properly – it is vital for decision making, keeping abreast of trends and picking up on potential problems or opportunities.

Moreover, maintaining good relationships makes dissatisfaction less likely and enables you to nip potential problems in the bud. Hidden agendas, personal resentments and hostile politics impede efficiency and can undermine management.

Finally, work is simply more enjoyable for all concerned when there is a spirit of co-operation.

Although this all sounds like common sense, many managers still retain the authoritarian, 'command-and-control' approach to running a team, feeling that it's necessary to instil fear. For such people, changing their managerial style will require tremendous personal effort and careful handling to avoid arousing suspicion that they have a hidden agenda. The effort will be well worth it, though, as the value of good relationships cannot be overestimated.

Remember: managers need to build up credit in the bank – you never know when you'll need to draw on it!

## How to build relationships

How you build relationships will rely a lot on your individual style, but here are some useful guidelines:

- Take time to establish rapport. Building good relationships is not an optional extra to be squeezed in whenever you have a few moments; it's a cornerstone of your success as a manager.
- Establish why you need a good relationship. Find a common objective, such as improving performance by 10 per cent, and focus on that. Remember that you're not building a relationship with a person just to be nice, it's in the interests of the business.
- Be patient – building a relationship takes time.
- Avoid being self-absorbed – focus on the other person. Rather than worrying about your image, whether or not the other person like you, or your own wants and needs, try to put yourself in their shoes. However, don't fall into the trap of assuming you know what's best for people, or what they want, without asking them. Listen carefully, and always check understanding and assumptions.
- Don't try to turn people into clones of yourself, and don't expect them always to have the same outlook as you. Try to develop your empathy and understanding. Team relationships work best when people are complementary – where there is a balance of skills, experiences and outlooks – not when everyone is the same.
- Don't merely *tolerate* differences, *exploit* them. This involves the following steps: identify the difference; allow for it; enjoy it; and finally, exploit it! This is, of course, far easier said than done. To exploit differences successfully, it's essential to focus on the benefits of the particular skills and qualities of each individual and the way in which they operate. It's also useful to recognize that this is a two-way process – the other person may also have difficulties with the way you work, and they too will need to learn how to gain from it!
- Be tolerant of people's weaknesses. Everyone has them – even you! Remember that a weakness is often the flip-side of a strength.
- Be open and master the art of feedback (see chapter 3, page 26, 'Helping others to achieve'). Don't put off tackling difficult issues – they'll only fester.
- Take genuine pleasure in other people and their success. Understand that, as a manager, their success is your success.
- If you're changing your behaviour or approach, explain your rationale, describing what you seek to achieve and asking for feedback. If you change overnight without explanation, people will be suspicious of your

motives – particularly if it's a one-off change, or your behaviour is inconsistent.

- Remember to *like* yourself and what you're doing, and behave in a way that ensures you will continue to do so. Not only will you sleep easier at nights, but other people will respond to your self-respect and integrity.

## Common mistakes

It's useful to be aware of some of the most common mistakes in handling personal relations.

Firstly, don't assume you automatically have rights over people. Good relationships are based on trust and respect, which you have to earn.

Another common mistake is being too eager. Rapport takes time to develop, and often there are barriers to overcome. What's more, no two relationships are the same – each develops at its own pace. So don't try to force it, and don't give up too soon – the breakthrough might be just around the corner.

You should also beware of taking things personally. 'I disagree' doesn't mean 'I think you're stupid' or 'I don't like you.' And 'I agree' doesn't necessarily mean 'I think you're brilliant' or 'I like you'! Remember, for the most part disagreements are about ideas.

Once you have established a good relationship, it's vital not to take the other person for granted. You must continue to show that you respect and value someone, if you want the same in return.

Finally, bear in mind that deception can shatter relationships. Ideally, you should try to tell the whole truth, all the time. Being open and honest establishes trust. However, there are of course times when complete honesty can do more harm than good, so be prudent and think about the possible impact of what you say.

---

This chapter shows how delegation, if handled skilfully, benefits everyone. Members of your team will have opportunities to learn and develop, and you will be free to concentrate on the most vital areas of your job. And you'll be less likely to end up with an ulcer!

Moreover, delegation can help you build relationships of trust, something that shouldn't be considered an optional extra. Good relationships don't only make work more fulfilling and enjoyable, they make for improved performance.

---

# 3 Helping others to achieve

**Could this be you?** I think I've assembled a good team – people seem keen to learn and to get results. If we could combine my experience and their energy, enthusiasm and ideas, we could really make an impact. They'd move ahead, our team would get results, and we'd all get the credit.

But somehow it doesn't seem to be happening. I need to bring my people on, steer them in the right direction and get them working to their full potential. But how?

Having accepted that you need the help of others in order to meet your goals, your role is to create an environment in which members of the team can perform to their full potential. This will involve:

- Providing individuals with performance objectives and the support and guidance they need to attain them.
- Facilitating the personal development of team members by helping them identify specific training and development opportunities.
- Encouraging people to be open, to make suggestions and to become more active in identifying the need for change – and allowing them to make mistakes.
- Boosting morale.

This chapter focuses in particular on listening skills, performance management and coaching.

## Active listening

A good manager needs to have his or her finger on the pulse. Productive relationships and communications with colleagues – and customers – depend on your ability to listen and interpret. To do your job properly, you should be spending at least half of your time listening to what other people say.

There will be benefits both for you and for members of your team. Money, time and energy will be saved if you can avoid misunderstandings by listening properly. And of course, you have to listen if you want to learn. Moreover, members of your team will feel more appreciated and so more motivated if it's clear you're interested in what they have to say.

Listening should be an *active* process, and never more so than when you're meeting someone for the first time, when your objective should be to say as little as possible and learn as much as you can in the shortest possible time.

Some people dismiss listening as automatic; others regard it as a skill that's easily acquired. In reality it's neither.

There are a number of important principles you need to follow to be a really effective listener:

- Find an uninterrupted area if possible and keep away from distractions, as they will spoil the flow.
- Be interested – you need to care about what people are saying if you are to improve your listening skills. Otherwise it will simply be too much effort.
- Silence your internal chatter and keep what you actually say to a minimum. Let the other person finish – often the core meaning is contained in the last few words. Avoid the tendency to finish someone's sentence for them, instead of listening to what they are actually saying. This is particularly important when you are in a familiar situation.
- Pay attention, and show that you are doing so by your body language – for instance by nodding and maintaining eye contact. This will put speakers at their ease. Remember that we rely on other people's facial expressions to tell us how we are faring in a conversation. The good listener doesn't look over someone's shoulder, or write while they are talking. If you have to take notes, explain what you are doing. Blame your poor memory, and make it clear that your note-taking is a tribute to the interest or importance of what you are hearing.
- Show support – express your interest and encourage others to continue.
- Check back – try to restate what the other person has just said, using their words as far as possible. This reassures them that what you heard is what they meant.
- Help the speaker to structure their ideas. Summarize and agree the main points before moving on.
- Build on the other person's argument – but don't use this as a technique to knock down their ideas and substitute your own.
- Listen with feeling as well as reason. Your main objective is to get inside the other person's head. If you were saying what they are saying, what might you really mean?

- Be alert to what the speaker is *not* saying. Very often what is missing is more important than what is actually there.
- Be aware of your personal prejudices and make a conscious effort to stop them influencing your judgement.
- Relax – research shows that tension reduces the effectiveness of our hearing.

## Performance management

Performance management brings company strategy to life by making clear the links between individual objectives, team objectives and company objectives. It will involve you in creating a shared vision of the purpose and aims of your organization; helping each team member understand the part they play in contributing to them; and enhancing the performance of team members by establishing objectives and monitoring progress (see also page 71, 'Appraisal').

### Benefits

Performance management programmes clarify individual responsibilities and accountabilities, and focus team members on what they must achieve. Additionally, by helping individuals to understand the business they're working in and how they fit in, such programmes increase motivation, work satisfaction and commitment. Recruitment and retention of staff should become easier as a result.

Improved communications are a related benefit. People will not only become aware of the objectives and plans of the organization as a whole, but will also have the opportunity to contribute to formulating them.

Performance management programmes also provide a good context for teamwork and coaching, and because such programmes define and measure standards of performance, they help identify objective criteria for recognizing and rewarding achievement. Overall, quality should improve.

### Key elements

Performance management is a flexible concept, but most programmes involve:
- setting performance objectives
- setting developmental objectives
- monitoring how team members are performing against the objectives set for them

## SETTING OBJECTIVES

It is important to set a balanced series of objectives to ensure that the business satisfies customers and achieves against traditional financial measures as well as developing individuals.

Don't try to set too many objectives – five or six will usually be enough. The approximate number may be set at the organizational level, but there is always room to be a bit flexible at a local level.

When establishing a programme, try to bear the following in mind:

- Objectives must be specific; identifying precisely what is going to be achieved.
- Objectives should be stretching enough for the individual to grow and develop – evidence suggests that performance improves as goals get tougher.
- Objectives must be mutually agreed *and understood*.
- If people don't expect to achieve, this can inhibit their performance. Some coaching may be required to overcome this.
- People perform much better if they have a strategy in place that will guide them towards achievement.

You should think hard about what constitutes good performance. It is not only what has to be achieved that matters (e.g. delivering an IT project on time), but also how it is achieved, (e.g. while maintaining good relationships with customers and those who will be using the system).

As a manager you need to strike a balance between capitalizing on individual flair and talents, and communicating clearly and fairly what your expectations of performance are. This is one of the reasons why discussion, agreement and understanding are vital in managing performance.

## MONITORING

The more frequently and regularly performance is reviewed the better – it is very unfair to set ambitious goals and strategies and then fail to provide adequate support and monitoring.

Begin by focusing on whether things are on track. If they are not, ask yourself what can be done to support the individual and help them get back on track. When trying to identify lessons to be learnt, focus on what has been achieved and what hasn't, and *why.*

Performance review should be in one-to-one sessions using as much support material – such as project plans, strategy plans and feedback from other colleagues and customers – as possible.

Feedback (see also page 69, 'How to provide effective feedback') is an essential part of managing performance – it helps people focus on areas they need to improve. It also encourages the transfer of ideas and information between team members. Too many good ideas and good working practices are lost simply because they are not shared.

Try to make feedback as specific as you can and, when giving negative feedback, be descriptive rather than making judgements. Stick to the facts and their consequences.

It's vital to accentuate the positive as well as giving constructive criticism. Maintain people's feelings of worth – those with higher self-esteem tend to react more positively to feedback. People often underestimate their own capabilities if they don't know how well they are doing, and here feedback can be used to set tougher goals. Team members should also be able to see a direct link between good performance and reward, so management in general should think about introducing performance-related pay and paying bonuses for good team and individual performance (see also chapter 14, page 104, 'Motivating people').

It's also crucial to allow individuals their say. As well as communicating expectations, you must work with someone to agree a way forward. Try to strike a balance between ensuring that people do what is required, and encouraging them to try new things that they themselves want to explore.

If goals aren't being met, in some instances the plan or objectives may need to be altered. But remember, working to changing agendas can be demotivating, and it is often the way a goal was going to be achieved that is inappropriate, so only amend goals as a last resort.

## Coaching

One-to-one coaching in the workplace is a tool for helping you to get the most from your people. It's a vital management function, and may well be something you are already doing naturally.

Every member of your team will benefit from regular on-the-job coaching. Without it, people may not be able to see how they can improve their performance. Good coaching can help individuals blossom and develop, acquire the right skills and attitudes, and become more creative and aware of the scope of their job and what constitutes success. Coaching sessions are also a good forum for agreeing plans and reviews.

A good coach encourages individuals to reflect on their performance and become aware of what they are doing and how they are doing it. Coaching should highlight successes and outline what improvements can still be made. This will help people become more skilful and reflective learners, so that they increasingly use their own experience as the key material for learning. In this way staff should gradually learn to monitor their own performance. At the same time, the coach provides essential information or knowledge to fill in any gaps.

If handled well, coaching will motivate the members of your team as well as helping them learn. They will see it as an aid to fulfilling their potential. In addition, it demonstrates your interest in their development and jobs, showing that you want to pay attention to them as individuals and can provide a point of stability in the face of constant change.

Overall, coaching should help to raise standards, bringing about a climate in which learning and innovation are both expected and rewarded.

## Principles of successful coaching

Coaching should:
- Be one to one.
- Start from where the person actually is in performance terms, not where they ought to be.
- Build on personal strengths and aim to remedy weaknesses.
- Be regular and involve constant feedback.
- Be person-driven rather than task-driven.
- Be a joint process.

The effectiveness of coaching depends on the skills of the coach and the receptivity of the person being coached, but success is most likely in conditions in which:
- There is clarity about job or role expectations.
- Success criteria are clearly established.
- Clear and regular feedback is given.
- There is some sense of the resources required to achieve targets.
- There is understanding of the work context.
- Rapport and trust have been established.

## How to conduct a coaching session

Here are some useful tips on the key stages in running a successful coaching session:

1 State the purpose and importance of the session – you need to be clear in your own mind about what you are trying to achieve before you begin.
2 Establish desired outcomes.

3  Give objective feedback. Ensure you pick up on any signals about how useful this is.
4  Identify the consequences of not addressing the problem or shortcoming.
5  Agree what the problem is and any resulting development needs.
6  Disclose your own feelings – demonstrate your faith in the person and your concern about the problem and the need to resolve it.
7  Seek suggestions for improvement. Explore what exactly is going wrong, and listen carefully – don't focus too much on whether what you are saying is right or not.
8  Build/clarify/discuss options. Ask questions, such as: 'Would it help to organize things differently?' or 'Are other people doing the same thing?' Don't only use questions that demonstrate your knowledge, or avoid questions to which you don't know the answer. Don't answer your own questions.
9  Agree development actions.
10 Check commitment.
11 Agree follow-up.

## Assessing your performance

The following exercise should help you assess how effective your coaching is.

Think back to your last coaching session (that is any face-to-face meeting that involved helping a member of staff to improve their performance or attitude, or develop skills).

How well did *you* perform? Give yourself a score of between 1 and 5 (1 = poor, 5 = very good) on all of the following:

| 1 | |
|---|---|
| Choosing the right place | ☐ |
| Investing sufficient time | ☐ |
| Providing the framework and defining parameters | ☐ |
| Mutually agreeing goals and the desired outcome of the session | ☐ |
| Clarifying where appropriate | ☐ |
| Summarizing where appropriate | ☐ |
| Agreeing review dates | ☐ |

## 2

| | |
|---|---|
| Building rapport and communicating openly | ☐ |
| Allowing the person to give an assessment of where they think they are now | ☐ |
| Listening actively and positively | ☐ |
| Asking for the person's thoughts and ideas | ☐ |
| Encouraging the person to take responsibility | ☐ |
| Using open questions | ☐ |
| Being open-minded | ☐ |

## 3

| | |
|---|---|
| Being assertive without being aggressive | ☐ |
| Building on the person's ideas | ☐ |
| Sharing your expertise (without being domineering or a know-all) | ☐ |
| Offering advice as needed | ☐ |
| Offering support as needed | ☐ |
| Giving clear, constructive feedback (positive and negative) | ☐ |
| Mutually agreeing performance goals | ☐ |

## 4

| | |
|---|---|
| Getting the person to admit there may be a problem | ☐ |
| Getting to the heart of the problem, not just the symptoms | ☐ |
| Managing any difficult emotions – your own and the other person's | ☐ |
| Identifying a range of solutions | ☐ |
| Jointly evaluating possible ways forward | ☐ |
| Agreeing the best course of action | ☐ |
| Building the person's commitment to take action | ☐ |

## ANALYSIS

The four sets of questions were grouped under numbers, which correspond to the topics below.

Fill in the scoring table for each topic, as well as computing the totals for the questionnaire overall.

| Topics | Total score for each topic | % score per topic (Score ÷ 35 x 100) |
|---|---|---|
| 1  Structuring | | |
| 2  Giving them a chance | | |
| 3  Giving your perspective | | |
| 4  Problem solving | | |

Calculate your overall score by adding together the total number of points you gave yourself for each topic, and converting it into a percentage by dividing that total by 140 and then multiplying by 100.

Ask yourself:

- Which topics hadthe highest score? And which the lowest?
- How do you feel about your results?
- How would the person have left the session feeling? Helped? Hindered? Or indifferent?
- Were there any specific examples of success or failure during the session which stick in your mind?
- If you could repeat the session, what would you do differently?

---

People need structure and support to perform at their best – and it's a manager's job to provide it. Your ability to bring on the members of your team is crucial to improving overall performance.

Time spent on listening to others, on performance management programmes and on coaching may not pay immediate dividends, but when they do come they should be substantial. The guidelines in this chapter will have put you on course to collect.

---

# 4 The art of influence

**Could this be you?** I thought that once I'd got the authority, it would all be easy. I try to give my boss what she wants, and I expect my team to do the same. But I'm beginning to see it isn't as simple as that. Just telling people to do something might get quick results, but you can't be sure they'll go the extra mile for you when it matters. Also, I need to persuade people across all kinds of functions – people who don't report to me. No, what I need is a way to influence people without making them feel pressurized. How can I persuade people that something is what they want to do themselves?

The authoritarian, 'command and control' approach to management is losing favour. Managers are now thought to be more effective if they persuade and influence, rather than relying on authority, power and fear.

Subtlety is the key. Team members, peers and bosses all need sensitive handling. If you are to get your way you need to be diplomatic, persuasive and convincing – in a word, influential.

Influence is all about getting people to listen to you, respect you and back you. It's about selling ideas, persuading people that your point of view is correct, and that what you want is what they want.

Getting people to change their minds or agree to something is quite an art, and you need to understand the processes involved in order to find the right strategies and avoid having to resort to coercion. But before we provide some guidelines, let's look at some of the areas you might be able to influence.

## What can you influence?

In our personal and professional lives, there are many things that concern us, but not all of them come into our sphere of influence.

Make a list of all the issues that concern you, such as your health, your family, problems at work, share prices and the environment. Separate these into two categories: things over which you have no control, and things you can influence. Then look at the two lists and ask yourself where you focus most of your time and energy.

Focusing mainly on areas over which you have little or no control is likely to result in blaming and accusing attitudes and feelings of victimization. You will also be neglecting areas you could do something about. As a result the number of areas you influence will shrink, reducing your potential to bring about positive change.

Categorizing issues in this way and thinking about how you direct your energies will help you focus more on things that you really can control or influence.

## Learning to influence

The first thing to remember is that you can't have influence without integrity. If you're selfish or act out of vested interest, people will always suspect your motives – trustworthiness is often judged by whether or not you have an axe to grind.

So far as tactics are concerned, there are three main approaches: consultation, persuasion and inspiration.

### Consultation

Simply announcing decisions tends to encourage disagreement and provoke challenge; you need to build your credibility and establish a reputation for being fair-minded and reasonable first.

If team members participate in planning and implementation, they will feel useful and respected, and will develop a sense of shared ownership of a project, strategy or change. As a result they will be more committed to making it a success.

So you should draw out others' contributions, building on and extending their ideas, rather than countering with alternatives. Open-ended questions (such as 'How would you see that developing?' or 'What would you expect the consequences to be?') should gently encourage people to see the value of what you are proposing. You should also be quick to give credit for others' ideas and suggestions, and be willing to delegate responsibilities, wherever possible. The more involved people are, the more they will feel they are working towards a shared goal, and the better the result is likely to be.

In addition, there should be fewer demands on you in terms of follow-up and supervision.

Consultation is especially appropriate if you have the authority to plan a task or project but are relying on other people to help implement the plans.

## Inspiration

Inspiration appeals to people's emotions, ideals, aspirations and values. It encourages personal commitment, and channels energy into working toward a common purpose. It is the most crucial element in your ability to sell an idea to others.

To gain commitment to a request or proposal, you'll need to show that it has exciting possibilities and generate a shared identity for your team – a common vision of the future. You then need to convince team members that through their collective and individual efforts this vision can become a reality.

## Persuasion

Persuasion involves the use of logical arguments, factual information, opinions and ideas. Its aim is to convince others that your request or proposal is feasible and consistent with shared objectives.

In order to persuade people, or sell them on an idea, you must be forward with your proposals and suggestions and not afraid of others' reactions to them. Effective persuasion requires persistence and energy.

With persuasion, the basis for agreement and approval is the soundness of your reasoning. Remember, the more important the issue, the more people will scrutinize your reasons, so be prepared!

You also need to cover all angles. The more arguments you can offer, the more likely people are to find at least one of them convincing. However, make sure each argument is sound, or you could end up weakening your position. You should also try to cover all the possible objections to your idea, and argue convincingly against them.

Persuasion is the most direct form of influence, and is most appropriate when you need to sell an idea to a large number of people.

## Getting it right

Your tactics are most likely to succeed if you:

- Choose an approach that is appropriate for the situation. Ask yourself what the best tactic or tactics will be, bearing in mind the guidelines above.
- Demonstrate that your proposals will benefit others, including people outside your immediate team. You'll get nowhere if you appear to be

concerned only for yourself or your team – people do things for their own reasons, not yours.

- Assure people that they are not being manipulated. If someone says 'I felt manipulated', it is not a compliment to your persuasive powers, it means they felt cheated, used or even deceived. Don't put upon people or treat them as an easy touch – they'll soon realise that they're being used and will turn against you.
- Try to make people feel good. If they do, they will then be more likely to make allowances, compromises and changes. When asking someone for something, try to catch them in a good mood, or introduce your request with a joke or light-hearted comment. When you make a request, appeal to someone's good nature, explain why it's important to you and make it clear you know you will owe them a favour.
- Understand and appreciate different people's values, and be sensitive to cultural differences.

In addition, you need to focus on your attitude, your communication skills and your approach to change.

## YOUR ATTITUDE

If you don't believe you can influence others, how do you expect them to believe it? You need to be confident that you can make things happen and deal with any obstacles within your control – don't waste time or energy on things you can do little or nothing about (see page 35, 'What can you influence?'). By acting and sounding like a winner, you are more likely to convince others of your power to bring about change.

Here are some examples of winner talk and loser talk:

| Winner: | Loser: |
| --- | --- |
| 'It's down to me.' | 'It's not my fault.' |
| 'We can change it.' | 'It's the system.' |
| 'We can find a better way.' | 'We've always done it like this.' |
| 'Let's find out.' | 'Who knows?' |
| 'I'm good, but I could be better.' | 'I'm better than some people.' |
| 'That's a piece of luck.' | 'That's typical of my bad luck.' |
| 'He/she has really done well. Good luck to them.' | 'He/she has really done well. It makes me sick.' |
| 'I'll do it if no one else can.' | 'Don't ask me – I only work here.' |
| 'I fell.' | 'Somebody pushed me.' |

## YOUR COMMUNICATION SKILLS

The way you present your case is critical (see also chapter 11, page 86, 'Communicating clearly'). If you mumble and hesitate, and your language is clumsy, you'll seem unsure of yourself, even if you're not. In addition, you should try to adapt your language for the person you're talking to. Repeating some of the other person's own words is a useful tactic, but this shouldn't be overdone. Draw the other person in by using 'we' rather than 'I' and 'you'.

You should also listen carefully to what others have to say (see page 26, 'Active listening'). Don't think about your reply or worry about the other person's possible reaction to what you might say, or complete other people's sentences for them, or allow yourself to be distracted by things around you. If you let others talk and show you can listen, you will encourage productive debate.

If you are giving a presentation, make sure your material and the technology you use will appeal to your audience. It's also important that your presentation doesn't suffer from Gloating Expert Syndrome. Check it for patronizing comments that might alienate people. Be focused – know exactly what you want to get across, and why. But be careful of putting across your point too forcefully – people might be suspicious of your motives and assume you simply have an axe to grind. Encourage the audience to participate.

## YOUR APPROACH TO CHANGE

If you are trying to introduce change, allow people to become familiar and comfortable with what you are proposing.

Remember the elements that help people adapt to change: providing information, offering involvement, giving support, reassuring people and guiding them through the process (see chapter 5, page 41, 'Thriving on change').

## Influencing a group

When you're a member of a group, additional factors come into play because people feel a strong pressure to conform. But have courage if you find yourself a lone voice – the majority isn't always right. Here are some guidelines for trying to influence a group:

- Try to recruit a few allies before a meeting.
- Present your arguments as confidently and clearly as you can. Show you can see the merits of others' positions, but explain why you feel yours is better.
- Talk a lot and talk sense. Contribute as much as you can to discussions,

showing you've done your homework and know exactly what you're on about.

- Don't put others down: stick to the issues.
- Don't feel overwhelmed. Remember, people tend to be impressed by those who have the courage to speak up for what they believe in.

---

Consultation, inspiration, persuasion – the key skills of the influential manager. And, as we have seen, influence is much more effective than command or coercion, because people don't resent it, and because it can be used with peers and superiors as well as with members of your team.

A manager with influence is a manager who really makes things happen. If you apply the principles outlined in this chapter, your reputation and your effectiveness will both grow along with your influence.

# 5 Thriving on change

**Could this be you?** Want to know the most over-used word in management today? It's 'change'. Sometimes I think that senior managers are just change junkies. As soon as you get good at anything, they throw something different at you. Of course we all have to make improvements, but what about the need to consolidate?

I know, though, that these days we all have to run twice as fast just to stay in the same place. I also know that unless we continually look at what we're doing, we'll fall behind. But I just find the whole process so unsettling – and it's clear my people do as well.

What's worrying me now is that I have to make some radical changes to my department. I feel sure it's all going to make my team feel very insecure and resentful.

Without evolutionary change, we would still be swimming around in the primordial soup. Change is the norm, not the exception – an essential aspect of human life, which creates new opportunities for growth and development, and challenges every individual to fulfil their potential.

We all experience change, both internally – physically, mentally and emotionally – and externally, in the ever-altering circumstances of our lives and the progress of the world around us. Change can be subtle and slow or sudden and dramatic, and it affects us everywhere: in the home, in our relationships, at leisure and at work.

Change can be an irrational and unpredictable process. It rarely conforms to a tidy pattern and often occurs in fits and starts. Major change and innovation is often the result of a leap of logic or the following of intuitive faith: witness the development and rise of Microsoft and the Internet.

Almost every aspect of management includes managing change. If you wish to harness the positive energy of change, you need to keep an open mind and be receptive. Change may seem threatening, evoking feelings of loss and loss of control. But like a caterpillar turning into a chrysalis, you have to experience a breakdown of the familiar before you can emerge as a butterfly. As change is inevitable, the healthiest approach you can take is to embrace it, work with it and, ultimately, make it work for you.

This chapter looks at how individuals react to change, explores some of the myths that surround it and offers guidance on how you can manage major changes more effectively.

## Change at work

Our increasingly complex and fast-moving world creates the necessity for constant change in business. Changing geographies, new environments, developing markets, increasingly fragmented consumer groupings, sophisticated technology, new legislation – all these elements and more require rapid appraisal and adaptation.

It's not as if change is anything new – it's always been a hallmark of successful organizations. But the pace of change has quickened. In business today, he who hesitates is lost. With both companies and individuals, whoever adapts most quickly to a changing situation will triumph.

Sometimes change will be planned (targets set, timetables for achieving goals established and progress monitored); sometimes it will be in response to a sudden change in circumstances (such as a drop in market share or a new product from a competitor). Either way consequences are uncertain, which is why the most successful managers need to thrive on uncertainty, not merely cope with it.

By not clinging to the belief that everything should be defined and definitive, and treating uncertainty and change as an opportunity rather than an inconvenience or aberration, you too can learn to thrive on change.

The best teacher in the subject of managing change is probably practical experience. However, there are some guidelines that will help you avoid common mistakes.

## Damaging assumptions about change

Your attempts to manage change will be more successful if you are aware of some damaging assumptions:

- *Managing change is an optional extra*. It is not – it's vital to the success of an organization.
- *To manage change is to control it*. It may be hard to accept, but the kinds of

changes that require real managing are often unpredictable in their outcomes.

- *Change happens quickly.* It's natural to hope for a quick solution once you have identified a problem. However, a process that involves changing deep-rooted habits won't happen overnight. Don't make the mistake of aborting new programmes that may be on the verge of working.

- *Solutions must be perfect.* If one enemy of change is giving up too soon, a still more formidable one has to be never getting started in the first place! This is a delaying tactic, pure and simple. If you wait until you have a perfect, all-embracing strategy, nothing will ever get done. In a change programme, you must expect to take the occasional step backwards in order to take two forwards. Minor setbacks don't matter – provided you're going in the right general direction.

- *Resistance is a bad sign.* On the contrary, it's when everyone seems happy that a change specialist becomes suspicious. Resistance is inevitable, as people question methods and evaluate what they are being asked to do. If they say they're enjoying the process in the early stages, you'd be wise to assume that they've found some way round it and aren't really changing at all!

- *Old dogs can't learn new tricks.* This is the most damaging assumption of all. The psychology of management is full of examples of people transforming their fortunes by taking responsibility for their own lives. Old dogs can prove surprisingly adept at learning new tricks when the rewards – either material, social, psychological or emotional – are clearly presented.

## A modern approach

The process of change is much less threatening now than it was 25 years ago. So much more is now known about what happens in organizations when they change that there's really no need for alarm – or much excuse for failure.

Most successful change programmes now start at the edge rather than at the centre of an organization – often in an individual factory, site, department or team, where they are led by managers who create new roles and responsibilities for their own people. The role of senior managers is to create an environment that spawns such initiatives, nurtures them, tolerates failures and publicizes successes across the whole organization.

Three quarters of change initiatives still fail or prove problematic, however. This is often because they are too rigid, or because they create emotional upheaval, lowering morale. In addition, changes tend to take longer than expected, and are often introduced when it's too late.

Successful change programmes are:
- flexible and evolutionary, continually monitored and fine-tuned.
- supported by the will, energy and commitment of everyone involved.
- instigated in time – not when an organization has already hit rock bottom.
- sustained for long enough to register results.

## Helping others to change

Individuals create and maintain change, and however large the organization, change is only effectively introduced by convincing individuals that it
is necessary and that it can be done. In practice, changing an organization
means changing a sufficiently large number of people in such a way that the
organization changes too.

Most people understand the need for change; if they are thoughtful,
they'll be more worried if their organization is *not* reviewing its way of
doing things! However, people's reactions vary according to their ability to
tolerate uncertainty, their sense of control and their trust. People also learn at
different rates, depending on their motivation and success, and this affects
the speed at which individuals adapt to change.

It's worth remembering the 1:1:1 rule: one third of a group will embrace
change, one third can be persuaded, and up to one third may never change.

### Introducing change

The way change is introduced is vital in winning the co-operation of others.
People need to be given time to get used to the idea of change. Moreover, as
individuals' work has an impact on the people around them, it is important
to give advance warning of changes to everyone who might be affected, not
only those who are carrying them out.

In addition, it is crucial to explain to people why they're being asked to
change, and to involve them in the planning process, so that they can make
contributions from their areas of knowledge and understand how they will
be affected. It is not enough just to tell them what is happening. Unless
people are involved, committed and prepared to adapt and learn, plans will
founder on the resistance they generate.

### Coping with resistance

Just as change is a natural part of life, resistance is a natural human
response! It can serve a useful purpose, providing an outlet for people's concerns, and you should encourage openness and make sure you listen sympa-
thetically.

The way resistance manifests itself will depend on the individual's personality, what happened in the past in a similar situation, what they know about the change and their feelings about the situation.

Resistance can take the form of active and open hostility, passive resistance, resignation or indifference. It can be due to self-interest, lack of trust, misunderstanding, conservatism and defensive attitudes. It may also be the result of uncertainty or disagreement about the facts, or of different assessments of the benefits of change. Whatever its cause, resistance always needs to be understood and taken seriously.

Change is an emotional issue, with people often required to abandon the habits of a lifetime. Often it's trivial details that cause the most trouble – moving someone to a new desk, or adding an extra responsibility that won't take more than five minutes a day.

But people grow attached to their own way of doing things. It may not be a particularly good habit, but at least it's theirs! People get scared as they think through the implications of a change programme. Some of the changes seem inconceivable: surely that could never work? They worry that the process of change will be unpredictable. They're right: it will be.

Your job is to reassure them that although what you are proposing may be difficult, it can and must be done, so their best policy is to get comfortable with new ideas rather than fight them.

It's a question of everyone being asked to make small adjustments, rather than a few people undertaking massive change. Because so many people are involved, you have to make allowances for the fact that they'll change at different rates, depending upon their style of learning, personality and motivation. Broadly speaking, the better someone is performing today, the more efficient they will be at picking up new ways of doing things tomorrow.

People don't resist change that they themselves want to make, so it's vital to make sure individuals feel valued and are actively involved. Show them how the change will benefit them.

Sometimes, of course, concerns or objections will be valid, in which case you can review and modify the process. Such feedback helps keep an organization in touch with what's really happening on the ground. It can also be an important source of innovation, encouraging people to find solutions to problems.

## Managing the process of change

As changes take place, people may pass through stages of shock, denial and disorientation before reaching grudging acceptance and finally commitment.

To help them develop this commitment, people are likely to need:

- information (I know what's going on)
- involvement (I'm part of this)
- support and reassurance (I can play my part, and it's an important one)
- guidance (I know what I'm meant to be doing)
- easy access to those in charge (they value my opinion)
- an opportunity to discuss how the process is affecting them (they care about me)
- clarification (they don't give me nasty surprises);
- respect for their values and dignity (I haven't been made to give up anything that's really important to me)
- hope (I know it's worth it – and we can do it!)

## What if it isn't working?

If your change initiative isn't working you should ask yourself what the reason might be, and whether you can do anything about it.

One possibility is that you've simply run out of steam. The implementation phase of a project lacks the glamour of the creative planning stage, so you have to be prepared for a sense of anticlimax and ready to nurse your team through the period of post-natal depression. Your brainchild needs to be kept alive until it develops a life of its own.

Another possibility is that you've run into a wall of conservatism. People may accept what you're recommending intellectually, but may be resistant emotionally to the consequences of implementing your programme. If this is happening, ask yourself if you have done everything you can to make people feel valued and involved (see above).

## Checklist for change

### PREPARATION

- Initiate diagnosis at all levels.
- Define new roles and responsibilities.
- Prepare a detailed training plan for the team. Involve experienced team members in training – this provides a challenge and increases their sense of responsibility.

### HELPING OTHERS TO CHANGE

- Explain changes well in advance, spelling out why they are important and how people will be affected. Provide as much information as you can.
- Foster consensus and involve people in the planning process.

- Balance persuasion with consultation and inspiration (see chapter 4, page 35, 'The art of influence').
- Listen to people's fears and try to answer them.
- Allocate new roles and responsibilities. Challenge people and make them feel involved in the process – participation reduces resistance to change, and encourages more creative problem solving.
- Make sure information, knowledge, skills and insights are shared, so that trust is built up, generating commitment rather than compliance.

## DEALING WITH RESISTANCE
- Show respect for others' values and dignity.
- Provide support and reassurance.
- Make sure individuals feel valued and are actively involved. Show them how the change will benefit them.
- Remember, resistance is not always simply an obstacle. People's doubts and concerns may be justified.

## MANAGING THE PROCESS
- Be flexible. Monitor and fine-tune continuously.
- Be available. Provide ongoing support and guidance, using your coaching and mentoring skills to the full.
- Don't overload key staff.
- Remind people of reasons for change.
- Don't give up too easily. Change takes time.

---

Change, then, is inevitable, and the pace of change is accelerating. Today's managers must therefore both embrace change themselves and learn to help others do the same. The key, once again, is involvement. If people are involved from an early stage, they will feel they have a stake in the process, and also that they have some control over it.

No one can pretend that change will not involve some stress and upheaval. But if change is well managed, people should also come to see it as a challenge and an adventure.

---

# 6 Creating an effective team

**Could this be you?** I've never assembled a team from scratch before, and, to be honest, I'm worried about it. So far, I've managed to ignore suggestions to get that pedantic fact-checker from Systems on board. And those 'creative thinkers' from Research and Development can forget it, too. I've got enough on my hands without trying to deal with people who clearly don't fit in. Obviously it makes sense for everyone to be on the same wavelength at the start – then there will be no need to worry about building team spirit and getting people off on the right foot.

Teamwork is about individuals working together to accomplish more than they could alone – and then sharing the rewards. A team harnesses, pools and exploits the strengths, skills and experience of its members, and so compensates for areas of individual weakness. One person's weakness is often another's strength; one person's ignorance, another's expertise.

Working life is too complicated to be negotiated comfortably by any one person acting in isolation. And working in a good team is exciting, stimulating, supportive, successful – and fun!

This chapter focuses on what you need to consider when assembling a team to perform a function or undertake a project (see chapter 12, page 93, 'Picking the right people').

## Types of teams

A team is any group of people who need each other to accomplish a result. They can be together on a long-term or short-term basis, with specific or general objectives, and with members drawn from diverse or similar backgrounds.

They come in a number of varieties, including:

- Functional teams – involving people from the same background brought together to achieve a specific objective, for example to redesign a manufacturing process.
- Project teams – involving members from various backgrounds who come together to achieve a particular task, for example to launch a new product or research a new market, and then split up. (See also chapter 17, page 123, 'Managing projects').
- Virtual teams – involving individuals in a number of remote sites connected by e-mail or video conferencing facilities, for example a national sales team whose members are based in a number of regional offices.
- Quality teams – involving individuals who come together specifically to make suggestions for improvements or implementing quality systems (see page 118, 'Quality').

In an effective team, members take genuine pleasure in each other's successes, support colleagues' decisions, and willingly take their share of the blame when things don't work out.

Teams also have other distinct benefits:
- They help people cope more effectively with change.
- They enable work and effort to be divided.
- They generate more possible solutions to problems.
- They minimize mistakes, as members can spot and correct each other's errors.
- They can increase motivation.

## Teams and groups

Teams are recognized as one of the best ways of ensuring that vital tasks in an organization are completed satisfactory. However, simply gathering a group of people to work together does not guarantee that they will work as a team.

If a team is not working effectively, its members act like hired hands and suggestions are not encouraged. Members may distrust colleagues and not feel appreciated. Disagreement is seen as divisive, so members are cautious about what they say and don't know how to resolve conflict. The ethos may be that it is more important to follow the crowd than to produce positive results.

If, on the other hand, there is genuine teamwork, no time is wasted struggling over territory – members feel shared ownership of the team. They apply their unique talents to team objectives, and feel free to express ideas and opinions. Disagreement is acceptable, and efforts are made to try to understand others' points of view. Conflict is seen as way of developing ideas and creativity. Members of a team participate in decisions and aim for a positive result

## Picking your team

When assembling a team you may be tempted to get your mates on board and create a group of like-minded individuals who can be relied on not to make waves.

This tends to create a cosy but not particularly effective environment. If all your people have roughly the same world view, your team is unlikely to grow or develop. Bringing together individuals with diverse views should improve the quality of decision-making, and will certainly increase versatility. A little criticism and disunity helps keep a team on its toes, and the right balance of personalities can make the difference between a winning and a losing team.

### Eight roles

The psychologist Meredith Belbin identified eight important roles – each requiring different characteristics – that need be filled to make a successful team.

#### RESOURCE INVESTIGATOR

Characteristics: extrovert, enthusiastic, curious, communicative.
Positive qualities: a capacity for contacting people and exploring anything new, with an ability to respond to challenge.

#### COMPLETER

Characteristics: painstaking, orderly, conscientious, anxious.
Positive qualities: a capacity for following through, perfectionism.

#### TEAMWORKER

Characteristics: socially-oriented, rather mild, sensitive.
Positive qualities: an ability to respond to people and situations and to promote team spirit.

#### MONITOR-EVALUATOR

Characteristics: sober, unemotional, prudent.
Positive qualities: judgement, discretion, hard-headedness.

### 'PLANT'

Characteristics: individualistic, serious-minded, unorthodox.
Positive qualities: genius, imagination, intellect, knowledge.

### SHAPER

Characteristics: highly-strung, outgoing, dynamic.
Positive qualities: drive, readiness to challenge things like inertia, ineffectiveness, complacency and self-deception.

### CO-ORDINATOR

Characteristics: calm, controlled, self-confident.
Positive qualities: a capacity for treating and welcoming all potential contributors on their merits, without prejudice and with a strong sense of objectives.

### IMPLEMENTER

Characteristics: conservative, dutiful and predictable.
Positive qualities: good organizing ability, common sense, hard work, self-discipline.

Ask yourself which categories your people fall into and whether or not you have a broad enough range in the team. Are you over-represented in some categories, and dangerously light elsewhere?

Although a well-rounded team needs to cover all the key areas, you don't have to have eight different people to carry out Belbin's eight functions. Choose your team to optimize performance: some people will be able to represent several different functions quite adequately.

## Six hats

Another way of introducing diversity and versatility into the team is to consider approaches to thinking. The different modes of thinking and their benefits are vividly illustrated by Edward de Bono's six thinking hats.

### WHITE HAT

White-hat thinking deals in facts and figures – it is neutral and objective. It has discipline and direction but offers no interpretations or opinions.

### RED HAT

The red hat is for emotions. It covers ordinary feelings such as fear, dislike and suspicion; and the more complex emotions involved in making judgements, such as hunch, intuition, taste and aesthetic feeling.

### YELLOW HAT
Yellow-hat thinking is positive and constructive, concerned with making things happen. It looks for value and benefits, and stands for sunshine, brightness, optimism and opportunity.

### GREEN HAT
Green-hat thinking is creative. The colour symbolizes fertility, growth and the value of seeds. It's an approach that generates new concepts and perceptions by breaking out of conventional patterns of thinking. The wearer of the green hat is primarily useful in the search for alternatives.

### BLUE HAT
Blue-hat thinking organizes the thinking process, defining problems and shaping questions. It is responsible for summaries, overviews and conclusions, monitors progress and sees that the rules are followed.

### BLACK HAT
Black-hat thinking identifies what is wrong – things that won't work, risks, dangers and design faults. The devil's advocate wears a black hat. Given our deep-rooted reluctance to look for evidence that contradicts our thinking, we can't do without the black hat.

The thinking hats are a useful device to make sure that everyone is in the right mental mode at a particular moment. For example, at the beginning of a big project, you'll want the team to have their green hats on. Before you make a final decision, however, someone must have scrutinized the various options with their black hat firmly in place.

## What a team needs to succeed
Here are the core requirements for a successful team:

### COMMON GOALS:
You must be clear about what you want to achieve, and how you propose to do it. A lack of clear goals results in misinterpretations, arguments, cross-purposes and apathy, and people may try to use the group to achieve personal goals.

By contrast, if the whole group knows what it's aiming for, people will show commitment and strive to achieve the team's objectives. Though the goals may change over time, each member should clearly understand what they are at any point.

### HIGH TARGETS:
You need to set challenging performance objectives.

### LEADERSHIP:
Whether leadership is traditional and hierarchical or shared, the team needs people who are respected and influential enough to get others to listen to them. Effective leaders are good communicators and know how to involve everyone, including those who are reluctant to play their part. Leaders should be able to co-ordinate work and build contacts outside the team.

Teams also need leaders with linking skills, that is the ability to unite the team and help it become balanced and cohesive. A good linker will strive to encourage respect, understanding and trust between team members. Communication skills are also important in this area: linking means listening to people's views before making decisions, being available and responsive to people's problems, and keeping team members up to date on a regular basis.

Involving team members in problem-solving on key issues is another way to keep morale, productivity and motivation high.

### INTERACTION/INVOLVEMENT OF ALL MEMBERS:
Involving all team members as equally as possible creates synergy, collective spirit and motivation, and ensures that the team fulfils its potential.

### MAINTENANCE OF INDIVIDUALS' SELF-ESTEEM:
Each person's contribution must be heard, valued and acknowledged. The challenge for the leader is to enhance self-esteem by avoiding favouritism and encouraging individuals to express themselves.

### OPEN COMMUNICATIONS:
In any group of people expressing opinions and ideas openly, there's bound to be some conflict. But if you try to stop people stating their views in order to suppress differences of opinion, you'll diminish their involvement in the team's work. The secret is to make your people feel confident that they can express themselves openly, without fear of ridicule or retaliation. However, you also need to make it clear that confrontation costs energy and effort – both of which might be better spent on the team's creative work.

You need to be aware of any factors that might inhibit discussion. For example, are there powerful members who stop conversation when they walk into a room? As a manager, it's up to you to encourage those who are inclined to be silent, and tactfully to rein in those who love the sound of their own voice.

Team members need to know that channels of communication are open, that they can speak their mind, share information, discuss issues, make suggestions and bring up new ideas. You also need to ensure that there is sufficient time allocated for discussion.

### DECISION-MAKING POWER:
Tasks should be centred around things the team has the power to influence. If its suggestions and output are ignored or vetoed, it is unproductive and demotivating.

### ATTENTION TO PROCESS:
From the outset, a team needs to be clear about how they are expected to complete a task – how the work will be structured and distributed, and the ground rules of working together.

Standard features of process you might consider include mechanisms for performance review, sharing information and making decisions.

### MUTUAL TRUST:
Trust can take years to build up and moments to destroy. You can avoid a lot of heartache by asking people to discuss at the outset the behaviours and attitudes they expect from others.

Problems are likely to emerge when commitments are not met, when a person betrays another's confidence or when team members are dishonest.

Other factors that can destroy trust include: different experiences, values and expectations, which colour people's attitudes toward others; competition for territory; and the imposition of goals and performance standards without prior discussion.

Trust and support should develop with time, provided people can talk freely about their fears, problems and limitations, and receive help and support from others.

### RESPECT FOR DIFFERENCES:
Members need to feel free to disagree and be different from others. When individuals' needs are not met, teamwork can be demotivating, so it is important for the leader to pay attention to this issue.

### CONSTRUCTIVE CONFLICT RESOLUTION:

Problems with internal politics and occasional flashes of bitchiness are part and parcel of office life, and you should accept this. But you should also intervene when things threaten to get out of hand. A gentle reminder that there's work to be done, and that you're not prepared to allow the team's work to be undermined by personality clashes or game-playing is generally sufficient.

Conflict over issues rather than personalities is not necessarily a problem – it plays a vital part in preventing complacency. And a devil's advocate can open closed minds to new ideas. If conflict is unresolved, though, it leads to resentment, lack of motivation and lower performance.

Overall, it's a question of balance: people need to be able to disagree and give and take frank criticism without resorting to personal attacks and losing respect for others. (See also page 62, 'Handling and exploiting conflict').

### COMMITMENT TO SOLVING PROBLEMS JOINTLY:

Finding solutions to complex or major problems is the biggest challenge for a project team. To succeed, team members must co-operate and pool their experience and skills.

### ROLE CLARITY:

Members need a clear understanding of what is expected of them and why their contribution is vital to the success of the team. Without such clarity, members may compete unproductively, duplicate tasks and become demotivated and confused. Roles must of course be matched to strengths and skills.

## Six steps to success

The following guidelines should help you set about getting a team off on the right foot in a methodical way:

### GETTING STARTED

- Even if the faces are already familiar, you should welcome people formally into the new team. If possible, arrange an event so that members can socialize together.
- Articulate a vision for the future. Establish clear objectives for the team, based on overall departmental objectives. Convey your vision to the team at every opportunity. (See also chapter 13, page 98, 'The vision thing'.)

### AGREEING THE BASICS

- Work out team members' roles and responsibilities. Make a chart so that everyone knows what everyone else should be doing.
- Ensure that any support teams also know who's who and where individuals will be working.
- Establish the immediate challenges and workload. Set clear objectives for the short term – then agree how these objectives will be met and what support or information you or other members of the team can provide.
- Agree reporting structures, routines and resource requirements.
- Explain day-to-day processes, such as approaches to decision-making, problem-solving and meetings.
- Explain how the team will be judged, and the performance criteria involved.
- Discuss what action will be taken if things don't go according to plan.

### ALLAYING FEARS

- Spend time with the individual members of the team to allow them to air their concerns about how the process has been handled up to now, and how things will pan out in the future.
- Explain why individuals' contributions are important, and their knowledge and expertise vital to the team's success.
- Gather suggestions on how to make connections and establish good relationships.
- Make it clear that you know mistakes happen, and that problems must be flagged up as soon as possible, so that the team can resolve them.

### ENCOURAGING CONTRIBUTIONS

- Work out which issues may be significant and encourage a collective plan of action from the whole team.
- Encourage team members to identify how they might best contribute to key areas.
- Help members understand more fully the different features and requirements of the business as a whole.
- Encourage repeated exposure to real problems – especially involving interactions with customers – as a way of developing the professional competence of team members.

### BUILDING TEAM SPIRIT

- Explain to team members how you expect them to work together and invite suggestions on how this can be achieved. Provide opportunities for the team to share and discuss ideas.

- Confront areas of conflict. In doing so, make sure everyone understands why this is important and focus on an approach that will help you resolve the issue.

## CHECKING EFFICIENCY

- Once your team is up and running, ask yourself whether any of the following statements seem apt:

'We're good on ideas, but weak on implementation.'

'We're not as co-ordinated as we could be.'

'We may be strong on the control side of the job, but we don't adapt well to change.'

'We need better back-up for our people in the field.'

'We never look at the wider picture.'

'We're very good at dealing with the task in hand, but lousy at addressing longer-term objectives.'

'We need to involve more team members in decision-making.'

---

This chapter has shown why diversity is vital to an effective team, and has given some guidelines on how to introduce it. It has also drawn attention to some of the other core requirements of a good team.

However, even if you've got the right people and established the right conditions, things can go wrong. The next chapter deals in more detail with some of the reasons why a team may not be working as well as it might, and suggests ways in which you can help.

# 7 Better team performance

**Could this be you?** I thought I'd done everything I could to make sure it worked, but I'm beginning to lose faith in this bunch of people – and in my ability to manage them. They all have different needs, strengths and interests, and somehow I have to look after all of them as individuals *and* get them to work together. I've set up weekly team meetings, but half of them wander in late, and they don't seem that bothered about contributing. Perhaps I'd get more out of them by talking to them one to one, or in small groups. How can I find a way of creating some enthusiasm and consensus?

uccessful teams accomplish tasks whilst maintaining or increasing their cohesion and willingness to work together.

If the approach to tasks is healthy, the team will be productive in the sense that the work will be done, people will take on responsibilities and members will share tasks according to their abilities.

If the social dimension is healthy, commitment and a sense of belonging will develop – individual members will feel good about working together.

Genuine teamwork takes time to develop. Teams don't work together automatically – sometimes a collection of talented individuals fails to gel, as many a football manager has found to his cost!

This chapter looks at some of the reasons why a team may not be performing to the limit of its potential, and introduces three ways in which you may be able to help the team improve: by developing your leadership skills, by finding new ways to resolve conflict, and by being a skilled facilitator.

## What's the problem?

It's easy to spot a team that's not working properly. Meetings will be unproductive. People will tend to look frustrated and sound grumpy, not only with their colleagues but with the very suggestion that they should all pull together. There may be a tense atmosphere overall, and people may be duplicating effort, working in isolation or competing in an unhealthy way. Team members will probably also have stopped being honest with each other, and will not admit mistakes. The chances are that the team is on a losing streak.

Teamwork can break down for many reasons, for example:

- Its members are too alike.
- Its members aren't utilizing their different skills.
- The team is too large.
- The team has been selected for an inappropriate task.
- The team is operating under impossible constraints.
- The team is badly led.
- There is too much – or too little – conflict within the team.

## Assessing team cohesion

This exercise should give you an idea of how well your team has gelled, and help you identify particular problems which are addressed throughout this chapter. Circle what you think the team would score against each statement, using the following key:

1 = Does not apply
2 = Rarely applies (about 20 per cent of the time)
3 = Sometimes applies (about 40 per cent of the time)
4 = Frequently applies (about 70 per cent of the time)
5 = Almost always applies (about 90 per cent of the time)

### TEAM MEMBERS:

1 Stay late, come to work early, or take work home to make sure a job gets done.
2 Attend regularly scheduled team meetings.
3 Successfully complete work assignments that were set by the team.
4 Try to improve the quality of the team's work.
5 Talk about their concern with the quality of the team's work.
6 Speak favourably about the team to others.
7 Help each other when necessary.
8 Go outside the team for help or resources when the team can't solve a problem itself.
9 Get to meetings on time.
10 Spend some free time with other team members.
11 Work hard to fulfil the responsibilities assigned to them by the team.

12 Remain positive when things don't go well for the team.
13 Talk enthusiastically about working together to achieve the team's goals.
14 Try hard not to let the team down.
15 Take on extra work when necessary to ensure that the team meets or exceeds its goals.
16 Want the team to be successful.
17 Are satisfied with the roles they have in the team.
18 Work to maintain a high level of team spirit and morale.
19 Take feedback about the team's performance seriously.
20 Think of themselves more as members of the team than as individuals.

If your score is less than 40 you've plenty of work to do to boost team cohesion; 40-70 indicates there is still room for improvement; whilst 70 or over suggests your team is functioning well.

## How to be an effective team leader

If your team is well balanced, with a variety of strengths and different personalities, you might question whether it really needs a leader. The simple answer is yes!

It's not enough simply to have a well-balanced team. Diversity breeds conflict, and conflict requires guidance to ensure that results are achieved and high performance ensured. Your role as a leader is to manage this aspect of teamwork. Because an effective team involves people with very different abilities and personalities, you'll need to be able to bring out the best in everyone without provoking accusations of favouritism or discrimination.

Also, as a team leader you must be strong enough to bring in new blood and ensure that the team is able to cope with the departure of key players.

Leaders are the medium through which goals are expressed, hopes and expectations channelled, and conflicts defused. They have to get to know everyone in the team – how much they value themselves, and how they can be deployed to best advantage.

Good leadership involves delegation (see chapter 2, page 18, 'You can't do it alone'), keeping an eagle eye on the team's objectives, and cultivating the helicopter vision that will give you a genuine overview of the situation.

The leader must recognize and exploit strengths within the team and be prepared to compensate for individual weaknesses. Though not everyone will have all the required skills all of the time, with effective leadership the composite skills of the team will be available to all of the team's members all of the time. Leading a team is a very different ball game from managing one-to-one, but leaders must be good at motivating individuals before they can expect to extract maximum value from the team.

In the modern business climate, you need to operate to a different set of principles than those traditionally associated with the manager's role, learning to accept team members as the experts, and developing your skills in facilitating, consulting, coaching and problem-solving.

Here's how the modern concept of leadership differs from the traditional definition of the roles of a manager:

| Leaders | Managers |
| --- | --- |
| Deal with change | Are concerned with stability |
| Have long-term perspective | Have short-term perspective |
| Inspire others with vision | Instruct |
| Ask about why | Ask how |
| Focus on corporate philosophy, values, and shared goals | Focus on tactics, structure and systems |
| Have 'helicopter' view | May not be able to see the wood for the trees |
| Empower team members (see chapter 16) | Control subordinates |
| Use charisma | Rely on authority |

As a leader, your aim is to create an environment in which team members share the responsibility for getting results. You must try to combine qualities that may at first sight seem contradictory, such as the need to be: intelligent, but not smug; forceful, but sensitive to other people's feelings; dynamic, but patient; an effective persuader, but a willing subscriber to other people's ideas; a fluent provider of information, and a good listener.

It is important for leaders to demonstrate to a team that they know where they want the team to go, how they are going to get there and what they expect each member of the team to achieve, but at the same time to invite suggestions and involve team members as much as possible in the detailed planning and implementation.

Here is a résumé of a leader's main responsibilities:
- To recruit the right people for the team
- To agree objectives and targets
- To emphasize the importance of teamwork
- To encourage participation
- To organize team tasks so members can co-operate and make their jobs easier

- To rotate jobs within the team so that members identify with the team as a whole, not just their own jobs
- To ensure that communications flow freely within and between teams
- To encourage informal meetings between teams to resolve problems
- To align the team's aims with the organization's overall aims and values
- To develop, guide, and support team members
- To provide direction and information
- To manage and resolve conflict
- To monitor team goals

## Handling and exploiting conflict

Team members must feel confident that they can express themselves openly, without fear of ridicule or retaliation. But they also have to recognize that confrontation is expensive in terms of energy and effort – both of which are needed for the team's creative work. The secret is balance.

Where conflict does occur, people react in various ways. They may try to avoid the issue – by minimizing the problem, procrastinating or dealing with the symptoms of conflict rather than its cause. They may square up and not give an inch. Or they may try to resolve the causes of conflict.

In the short term, it may be possible to pursue one or both of the first two alternatives. Eventually, however, the conflict will have to be resolved – not just to make things happen, but in the interest of organizational harmony.

There are three possible approaches to resolving conflict:

• **Peaceful co-existence**: The aim here is to reformulate the problem, playing down differences and emphasizing common ground. The problem is that this may be tantamount to avoiding the issue. This solution is more applicable to personality clashes, though even here there may well be difficulties – false bonhomie doesn't last, and the real issues will probably surface again.

• **Compromise**: Negotiating so that neither side feels that they've lost appeals to pragmatists more than to idealists. The assumption is that there's no ideal solution, and once again the real issues may not have been resolved.

• **Genuine resolution**: This involves trying to find a genuine solution to the problem rather than merely accommodating conflicting points of view. The atmosphere of conflict and tension can be exploited to galvanize people into thinking again, trying fresh approaches, considering new ideas and creating a new dynamic of co-operation and discussion. Alternatively, people can take disputes to other members of the team – someone with a wider perspective on the situation would be ideal.

## Facilitation

Facilitation is the art of steering a team discussion to enable those present to get the most from each other and make debate as productive as possible.

It involves creating an environment in which people focus on the key issues, listen to each other and contribute effectively with the objectives of the team meeting clearly in mind. If you achieve this, you'll be helping to motivate and inspire commitment and action in others.

To be effective, you'll need to manage three crucial elements of the team meeting simultaneously:

• **The *feelings* of the people present**: Are the members of the group committed? Bored? Tired? Hostile? Co-operative? What can you do to create a healthier atmosphere? Would it help to call a break or change the approach? How can you keep people active and involved? What can you do to reduce conflict (see below)?

• **The *process* to which the group is working**: Would breaking up into subgroups help people focus on the issues more clearly? Are they sticking closely enough to the agenda? Would a brainstorming session open up new avenues to explore?

• **The *content* of the debate**: Are people learning from each other? Are they sharing information? Are they solving problems? Are they simply re-hashing old ideas?

### Facilitation skills

Before any team meeting or get-together, the facilitator needs to think about what the team is trying to achieve, what stages they will need to go through to get there, and what kind of information needs to be discussed or uncovered.

The point of most facilitated sessions is to elicit and organize information in a way that helps a team get to the heart of whatever issues it is facing – to help them diagnose the situation and determine what action needs to be taken. Often just posing the right question for the team is the most effective tool.

When planning a team session, the key is to keep every element of the process tied clearly to your overall objectives, so make sure these are clear in your own mind, and that they inform your thoughts on how you will set the scene, what questions you will ask and what techniques you will use.

As a facilitator you'll need to switch between the following modes:

- **Observing**: paying attention to people's body language, exchanges of looks, facial expressions, etc. Remember to look at those who are listening as well as those who are talking.
- **Assimilating**: As well as listening carefully to what is being said, it's your role to help the group assimilate what has been said or agreed, by summarizing or paraphrasing, or by inviting others to do so.
- **Intervening**: At times you'll also need to intervene in the discussion more directly, to steer it back on to the right track or resolve conflict.

Here are some guidelines on the key issues for a facilitator:

### INITIATING DISCUSSION
Set the scene, clearly stating the objective and asking for contributions from everyone. Explain your role at the outset: you are there to guide the process of the discussion.

### RECORDING INFORMATION
Encourage team members to use flipcharts to highlight, summarize and collect discussion points. Depending on what you are going to do with the information afterwards, keeping notes or using audio tape might also be appropriate.

### TIME-KEEPING
Put a time limit on each item and explain the importance of keeping to these times if the agenda is to be covered.

### PERSONAL ATTACKS
Make it clear from the outset that these will not be tolerated. Be careful not to crush people yourself – acknowledge all contributions, even those which aren't strictly sensible!

### CONFLICTS
If you can, nip arguments in the bud by anticipating sticky patches, focusing disagreements back to the centre and reiterating the difference between feuding and disagreeing – only the latter leads to a constructive outcome. If arguments persist, you might want to take a vote, or give each side a limited platform to state their case. (See also page 62, 'Handling and exploiting conflict'.)

## LOUD OR OVERBEARING TEAM MEMBERS

Balance the views of the more vociferous by coaxing those who are less forward. Bring everyone into the discussion. Be on your guard for any kind of intimidation, particularly when female members are outnumbered and challenged by males of higher status/power.

## WAFFLING OR MOVING OFF THE POINT

Gauge the usefulness of discussion and bring people back to order if they drift from the point. Integrate ideas where possible and remind the group that they are there to make progress.

On the other hand, you should be sensitive to the needs of the team and prepared to move the goalposts if necessary: should the members clearly not want to talk about the issues originally identified as the subject of the meeting, it might be productive to let them air what concerns them most.

## PLAYING DEVIL'S ADVOCATE

When you see the team conforming on a major issue without questioning it, pose an alternative argument. It might be a good idea to have each member act as 'critical evaluator' to bring hidden doubts and objections to the surface.

## DIFFICULT QUESTIONS

No one can be expected to have answers to every question raised. If you can't answer a particular question, throw it open to the group. If no one knows the answer, make a note of it so that you can find the answer later.

## SUMMARIZING

Paraphrase what team members have said to you: this will ensure that you have understood what they meant. Recap and summarize the key points, so that everyone has a clear picture of what has been said and where you are in the discussion. Finally, review each topic when it has been discussed, if possible ensuring a firm conclusion is reached. Record conclusions for all to see.

## ACTION PLANNING

Emphasize the importance of action planning. Without a collective effort to make plans to act on the results of discussions, meetings are little more than talking shops.

**Remember:**
- Be supportive
- Listen actively (see chapter 3, page 26, 'Helping others to achieve)
- Question critically
- Clarify issues
- Summarize progress

## VERBAL TECHNIQUES

You may find the following verbal techniques useful (see also chapter 11, page 86, 'Communicating clearly').
- Pay attention to your tone and volume: a voice that encourages participation displays confidence and enthusiasm; is clear but not overpowering.
- Ask open-ended questions: 'What is your reaction?' 'How can we improve?'
- Phrase requests to encourage more responses: 'Describe the process you used.' 'Tell us more about that.'
- Respond positively to participants' contributions: 'Good point.' 'That's a fresh perspective.'
- Ask for more specifics: 'Could you be more specific?' 'What do you mean by that?'
- Ask for and encourage different points of view: 'We have only discussed one or two viewpoints. Are there any others on this subject?' 'Is there anything we haven't thought of?'
- Redirect questions: 'What do the rest of you think about that?' 'Someone here must have a response to that?'
- Paraphrase: 'If I understand correctly, you're saying...'
- Refer to contributions people have made: 'That relates to Joe's earlier comment about...'

## NON-VERBAL TECHNIQUES

There are a number of non-verbal techniques you'll also need to master.
- Attentiveness: Pay attention to the person who is talking. Establish good eye contact, relaxing your posture, and turning towards the speaker.
- Silence: Silence is a critical tool of a good facilitator. Good listeners know when to pause, wait and say nothing. (See also chapter 3, page 26, 'Helping others to acheive'.)
- Movement: Standing fixed in one spot with hands and arms rigidly in the same position is not a good idea. Stiffness conveys tenseness and nervousness, so it is better to move about in a relaxed manner or to sit down than to stand in one spot.

## Avoiding common mistakes

There's no template for a good meeting. Facilitators must adapt to different circumstances and different groups. But there are some common errors that you should try to avoid in all situations.

Firstly, try to avoid any temptation to play the expert. You are not expected to be the source of all knowledge on the topics under discussion, and you don't have to provide answers to all the questions. Your role is to help the team find answers. If you don't know the answer either say so, or ask the delegates what they think, or both.

It's important to avoid imposing your own view on debates, or monopolizing the discussion. You may feel it appropriate to give your view; you may be asked for it. But always remember that the discussion should primarily be between the other participants.

On the other hand, you should make sure you don't lose control of the *process*. Don't let the discussion get bogged down in details, and if individual delegates seem to be in danger of disappearing down a side-track, come in firmly and guide them back to the central issues.

So, though the emphasis these days is on vision and facilitation rather than authority and control, a team leader must take an active role if a team is to succeed and carry on succeeding. It's a role that requires application and patience, but the practical guidelines in this chapter will help you create the right circumstances. And the effort will certainly be worth while – when people are working closely together, sparks may fly, but the results can also be scintillating.

# 8 Telling people what you think of them

**Could this be you?** I asked my team for feedback on my performance – and apparently I don't give them enough feedback! And when I do tell them what I think of how they're doing, they say I go completely over the top and it comes like a bolt from the blue.

The truth of it is, I find it really hard to give feedback. I feel very uncomfortable confronting people about problems and only do it when it's absolutely necessary. The feelings have usually been bottled up for so long that they come out in a bit of an explosion. I often end up shouting at people without meaning to, and only realize the damage I've caused when it's too late. As for praise, surely it's patronizing to congratulate someone for doing what they are paid for.

People can't be expected to improve unless they know what they're doing well, adequately or badly, and why. And people can't be expected to work this out in a vacuum – unless they're told otherwise, they will naturally assume that they're doing everything right.

The way in which you provide such information is vital if it's to be constructive and not lead to resentment and loss of motivation. This chapter focuses on how you can improve individuals' performance by giving continual constructive feedback, and through more formal systems of appraisal.

## Feedback

Feedback is a way of helping individuals to change their behaviour and keep on target to achieve their goals. It lets people know how well their behaviour corresponds to what you had in mind, as well as making team members more aware of what's required, what's expected and what skills they may need to acquire.

Feedback can also enable people to see things about themselves that they wouldn't otherwise recognize, and provides essential information to help them enhance their positive qualities and focus on areas that need to be changed. Highlighting and rewarding good performance is just as important as pointing out where people are going wrong. Even if someone is performing well, without feedback they may not be aware of it and may lose motivation. By explaining how peoples' performance affects others, and by comparing past and present performance, feedback can create a sense of achievement and accomplishment, which in turn can lead to improved and more creative effort.

Overall, good feedback creates an environment in which anything is seen to be possible.

## How to provide effective feedback

If people perceive themselves to be under attack they may resort to a number of different tactics to deflect criticism, for example:

**Defensiveness:** 'I'm not the only one who does that – why pick on me?'

**Resistance:** 'There's no way I can change – why should I?'

**Denial:** 'I didn't do that.'

**Excuses:** 'That wasn't my fault, because...'

**Pre-prepared arguments**: 'I knew you were going to bring that up. Well, let me tell you my side...'

**Attack**: 'What about you – do you think *you're* perfect?'

**Taking it personally:** 'Is *this* what people have been thinking about me? I thought they liked me.'

**Refusing to listen:** 'Here we go again.'

**Distrust of the person/process:** 'It's obvious – someone's got an axe to grind.'

**Masking true feelings:** 'I don't care what you say about me.'

**Concentrating on the person behind the feedback:** 'I bet I know who said that.'

Here are some guidelines to giving feedback so that it is seen to be helpful and not resented:

• Pick an appropriate time and place.

• Be specific. Being told you are too negative is not as useful as being told: 'When we were discussing an issue, you did not come up with any positive suggestions.' Equally, if you're praising someone's performance, it's important to give examples.

• Give the feedback in sequence. Your comments should progress from measurable performance (for example, 'This project didn't meet these objectives') to personal insights (for example, 'I don't think you spent enough time on planning') to the consequences (for example, 'So people didn't know exactly what to do or how to do it').

- Don't base feedback on hearsay and gossip. Always find facts to support your arguments.
- Consider the needs of the person receiving the feedback. Feedback can be destructive if it takes only your needs into account. It should benefit the recipient, not be an ego trip for you.
- Check to ensure you are communicating clearly. Ask the other person to rephrase what you have said to see if it is what you meant.
- Concentrate on your pitch and tone so valuable information is not perceived as complaint, criticism, or nagging. Beware of sounding patronizing.
- Balance negative feedback with positive feedback. Take any recent changes or improvements into account.

## Handling negative feedback

Negative feedback is the most difficult to give and receive, but it's a critical part of the learning process. Here are some tips on how to make criticism constructive:

- Explain why what you're discussing is important.
- Be specific and give examples. This is particularly important with negative feedback.
- Describe rather than evaluate. Concentrate on the facts – what happened in a particular situation and the consequences. You could use your own reactions to illustrate the consequences of a person's behaviour: 'I felt let down,' rather than 'You let me down.' Avoiding evaluative language makes it less likely that an individual will react defensively.
- Direct your remarks towards specific skills or actions that can be improved or changed, not towards personality characteristics an individual can do little or nothing about. For example, it might be helpful to suggest that someone should improve their presentation skills, but it wouldn't be much use simply to say 'You're too introverted.'
- Seek solutions. Rather than attributing blame, focus on the way forward – discuss what can be done and include suggestions for improvement.
- Don't put it off! Delay can only make it worse.

## Constructive and destructive criticism

It's vital to distinguish between feedback and censure, which is designed solely to knock people down, without any consideration given to building them up again.

**Feedback** is information designed to help people change their behaviour in a positive way. It is clear, specific and descriptive, and tough on issues not on people. It is also forward-looking and concentrates on finding solutions rather than attributing blame.

**Censure**, on the other hand, is a way of dumping your anger and trying to force people to conform to your idea of what they should be. It tends to be general and evaluative, and tough on people rather than issues. It also tends to concentrate only on the past – on attributing blame rather than finding solutions.

## Appraisal

Appraisal is a more formal way of providing feedback, occurring perhaps once or twice a year.

Appraisal provides an opportunity for you to learn about the career aspirations and plans of your team members, and allows them to learn what you think of their overall performance. Areas to cover include personal development, teamwork, contribution to the organization's goals and promotion prospects.

The point of appraisal is to improve performance – if performance is not improving, you should start to worry, as nothing and no one can stand still and remain successful.

Remember that appraisal of an individual's performance cannot be carried out in isolation from the overall activities, values and direction of an organization. When individual performance is measured, it should be in the context of adding value and quality to the whole organization, not just completing tasks or doing them a little quicker.

A method called '360-degree' appraisal is becoming increasingly popular. This involves gathering feedback from a number of different sources who have differing perspectives (including both more junior and more senior colleagues). This type of appraisal gives someone a more complete and balanced picture of how an individual's performance is viewed.

### How do appraisals work?

Appraisals influence and change behaviour by:
- providing feedback
- communicating standards of performance and/or behaviour expected of team members
- developing and coaching
- enhancing teamwork
- strengthening self-esteem
- reinforcing a sense of direction
- setting goals

## What's involved?

A successful appraisal:

- is a two-way process
- focuses on how results are achieved and on the skills required for people to perform effectively
- focuses on behaviour rather than perception
- involves your earning the right to criticize
- monitors results
- results in *agreed* goals

It's important to remember that results may be bad for reasons beyond the control of the individual concerned – for example if inadequate support or resources are provided.

Identifying and assessing the skills needed to produce results is as important as making people accountable for poor performance. Measuring actual results is relatively easy; measuring competencies is much harder and invariably involves more time. Focusing on *how* results are achieved can tell the appraiser why results are poor, acceptable or exceptional, and what can be done about it. Skills such as decision-making, communicating and negotiating have to be carefully observed at first hand, and feedback in these areas must be supported by specific, factual examples.

Some relevant skills will be general; others will be specific to an individual job. Either way, once they are identified *and agreed*, you must discuss what the skills involve in practice and provide advice and coaching where necessary.

Goals should be specified as clearly as possible, with measurable criteria established to enable appraisal to be as precise and objective as possible. Agree with the team members the methods you will use to measure improvement – observation, feedback from clients, feedback from colleagues, and so on. Objectives should be renewed every six months or so to see if they need amending.

## Conducting an appraisal interview

Appraising is as much to do with how the appraisal is carried out as what is actually appraised.

The appraisal interview itself should be a discussion, involving a sharing of information that has already been obtained and feedback of positive and negative points on behaviour and performance.

Here are some key points to remember when conducting the interview:

- Concentrate feedback on the facts – on what has actually been observed. Avoid feedback based on opinion or feelings.

- Be specific – general statements that attempt to cover performance as a whole are unhelpful.
- Avoid over-kill.
- Keep the feedback relevant to agreed objectives – there is a limit to what can be tackled in terms of improvement.
- Limit the feedback to areas the person being appraised can do something about.
- Avoid criticism that is likely to be taken personally.
- Speak plainly – do not use jargon.

Here are nine steps that will help you conduct a successful appraisal:

1. Ensure you are adequately prepared. Select an appropriate time, date, and location.
2. Begin by putting the job holder at ease. Show some interest in the person being appraised, then explain the process and introduce and check the objectives and measurement process agreed at the last appraisal.
3. Review the competencies and skills associated with the job – and agree your objectives for the next period.
4. Evaluate any numerical or quantifiable targets.
5. Discuss the individual's skills and technical knowledge (including on systems and processes), exploring problems and giving feedback.
6. Encourage comment on any factors beyond a person's control.
7. Agree development needs and a plan of action.
8. Explore career aspirations.
9. In the spirit of practising what you preach, get feedback on how the appraisal was carried out.

---

So, giving honest feedback may not be something that comes naturally to many people, but avoiding it can be disastrous. It's extremely discouraging for the members of your team to feel that they're working in a vacuum – that you don't really notice or care how they're doing.

However, as we've seen, feedback must be handled with great care. If there's one thing worse than working in a vacuum, it's the feeling that your team leader constantly criticizes you and puts you down. This chapter has given some practical advice on how to make feedback constructive, so that it not only improves the performance of individuals and teams, but also helps foster a positive working atmosphere and job satisfaction.

---

# 9 Managing customer relationships

**Could this be you?** Overall, my team seems to be doing well. We're reaching our monthly targets, and we've got the best attendance record in the department. But I've got a problem. Apparently, some customers have written in to complain about the way they've been treated. What's more, I've seen it for myself – customers being passed on to another department, left on hold till they hang up.

Some of my people just don't seem to be able to see a problem from the customer's point of view at all. As they see it, they're just getting on with their job as well as they can, and customers don't appreciate the pressure they're under. I need to show them that customers matter, and that without them, there simply wouldn't be a job at all. But how can I change their attitudes and priorities?

Customers matter. If you don't satisfy your customers they will simply go elsewhere for the products and services your company currently provides. Just think about how much your customers have spent over the last few years; now imagine what business would be like if they disappeared overnight!

As a manager, you have a critical role to play in delivering excellent customer service. Obviously various distractions (for example, the desire for promotion, pleasing your boss, managing the sheer volume of work, planning ahead) will intervene; but whilst this is understandable it is certainly not acceptable. In a business environment characterized by unpredictability, risk and impossible timescales, companies are increasingly recognizing the importance of building long-term relationships with customers.

This chapter examines how you and your team can improve service delivery by becoming more focused on the building of stable and rewarding relationships with customers.

# The importance of customer service

We are all customers ourselves, and know instinctively when we're getting good, bad or indifferent service. These days most managers can talk fluently about customer service and customer needs, and are well versed in the penalties of getting customer relationships wrong as well as the benefits of getting it right.

They know that customers who are very impressed with service are more likely to re-purchase, return or recommend than those who are merely satisfied, and that companies with excellent customer service are able to charge higher prices for their products.

They might not know that:

- Companies can boost profits by almost 100 per cent by retaining just 5 per cent more of their customers.
- It costs 5 times as much to get new customers as it does to retain existing ones.
- Dissatisfied customers have big mouths; the average person who has a bad service experience tells at least 9 others about it (compared with 3 or 4 others if they receive excellent service).
- If a complaint is resolved 70 per cent of customers will do more business – resolve it quickly and that figure grows to 90 per cent.

Despite all this, you regularly see examples of companies squandering their reputation and profitability by treating customers badly at every level. Common sense is probably the hardest thing to introduce into a business. A reluctance to act is to some extent understandable; good customer relations can mean more work. Asking customers what they want introduces more demands and more variables into a business. And, of course, there will undoubtedly be some bad news to handle.

In addition, there are many barriers to overcome in changing people's attitudes and behaviour. Organizations are full of people who are concerned with money, with power, with promotion, with careers, with battles between departments – with a whole range of things that distract them from satisfying customers. Let's be honest – it's hard to be positive with an angry customer if you've just been told you're not receiving your annual bonus!

However, it's your job to ensure that customers come back, so any value that you can add in terms of customer service is a vital element in helping your company compete.

### Becoming more customer service focused

Traditionally, organizations have been structured with the boss at the top of the pile, with all the attention and efforts focused on keeping him or her happy. In contrast, customers are at the bottom of the heap. When confronted with a choice, a customer-facing employee would always satisfy their boss before satisfying their customer.

Communication in this type of organization tends to be one way only – from the boss down – with little opportunity for people who deal with the customers to pass issues back up the line to senior staff. Thus, customers are often blamed or ignored and may become 'difficult' as a result, while front-line staff tend to feel isolated.

It is hard to take risks in this type of organization, because the focus is on apportioning blame rather than on giving staff what they need to provide good service to customers. Everyone may think they know what is happening, but what they know is often based solely on subjective opinion; there is no objective measurement of what's happening.

Some characteristics of an oganization like this include:

- Being inwardly focused, self-absorbed, pre-occupied and political.
- Management suppresses or restricts information because access to it is regarded as a source of power.
- Bad news (especially from customers) is usually greeted with blame from the top.
- Stress abounds due to constant efforts to meet the political requirements of the organization.
- People are good at avoiding getting stabbed in the back and often  blame their failures on other people. They only seem to be happy when they are able to push the blame somewhere else.

In the alternative type of organization (one that you should be aiming for) the focus of everyone in the company is on improving the service received by customers. Managers actively look for ways to help their people give excellent service to customers. There is good communication up, down, and across the organization, and staff who deal with customers feel involved and valued.

Customers are more likely to get the service they want, because everyone who works for the organization is encouraged to take responsibility for customers' needs.

Characteristics of organizations like this include:

- Being outwardly focused and aware of staff and customer needs.
- Managers see their roles as facilitating the flow of information because

they believe that information is knowledge. They genuinely feel that the biggest risk to the organization is keeping quiet about problems.

- Stress is caused only by efforts made to maintain customer satisfaction and keep apace of change.
- People are good at identifying gaps in customer service and feeding customer information back into the organization, and are happy when they can see the fruits of their efforts, i.e. satisfied customers. Satisfied customers result in smoother working relations all round!

## How customer focused are you?

This short quiz will provide some insights into your attitude towards customers. Read the following statements (ignoring any which are not relevant to your job) putting 'A' if you agree with the statement and 'D' if you disagree:

1  Complaints are the one thing I dread in this job. ☐
2  I generally take full responsibility in my job; the buck definitely does stop here. ☐
3  I can't concern myself with every customer's problem, otherwise I'd never get anything done. ☐
4  Sometimes I ignore customers who look like they need help. ☐
5  If a customer has a go at me, I try very hard to keep my cool. ☐
6  There's no point seeing customers as the enemy – without them, we'd have no jobs. ☐
7  There's no point using your discretion. There's always a rule that stops you. ☐
8  It's best to solve problems as quickly as possible, otherwise they just fester and get worse. ☐
9  I always try to be one step ahead of the customer in terms of what they need. ☐
10 If I can't give a customer what they want, I always try to give them an alternative. ☐
11 If you admit to being wrong, you're in trouble right away. It's always your fault. ☐
12 Not all customers complain for the fun of it. Most of them have real problems. ☐
13 If a customer is difficult and unreasonable with me, then I'll be difficult back. ☐
14 You can never really win an argument with a customer. ☐
15 It's not my job to, but I would help a customer ☐

16 Customers have no common sense - they always ask the obvious. ☐
17 I'll always take a bit of extra time to make things easier for
other people in the organization. ☐

If you put an 'A' against statements 2, 5, 6, 8, 9, 10, 12, 15 and 17 then award yourself 2 points for each. Also award yourself 2 points for every 'D' you placed against statements 1, 3, 4, 7, 11, 13, 14 and 16. If your score is 0-20 you've got plenty of room for improvement; 20-30 means you are well on the way to being customer focused; 30+ you possess genuine customer focus.

## How to improve your service to customers

Here are some of the ways in which you can help improve customer service and relations:

- Demonstrate your commitment to customers at all times.
- Keep the customer at the top of the agenda (even to the extent of being boring about it).
- Resist clichéd, negative reactions to customers.
- Attempt to change the behaviour of members of your team for the better.
- Drive out fear – of trying something new, implementing new ideas, the future, and failure.
- Encourage employees to share their successes and best practice.
- Measure performance and trends of those who work for you – making it clear exactly what you are looking for.
- Try and eliminate the 'not invented here' syndrome.
- Be aware of what your team members are doing.
- Acknowledge successes in team briefings – maybe even giving awards for outstanding service.
- Praise those who provide good customer service.
- Build your systems around your customers. Good customer service depends on quality systems (see page 118, 'Quality') as well as personal service. Make access easy for the customer, give a fast response, and try to demonstrate that systems are designed for the customer (invoices and forms, for example, must be user-friendly and easy both to read and to comprehend). The more high-tech the systems are, the greater the need for the personal touch. Remove any defects and bugs from your systems. If the systems hinder anyone, change them.
- Stay in touch with how customers are being treated: make sure you don't neglect MBWA (management by walking about!).
- Establish direct contact with customers and request feedback from them, by talking to them directly, or by such means as providing an e-mail

address or phone line specifically for the purpose. Encourage dissatisfied customers to complain – at least you'll then know that something is wrong and can try to do something about it.

- Learn from your mistakes: customers must feel that what they say actually makes a difference, and that canvassing their opinions is not just window-dressing.
- Compare your practice with that of others, both within your company and outside.
- Establish benchmarks by going to see how other businesses are doing it. Don't be fooled into believing that you've fixed it for good. Experiment – try out new approaches to see if they can make a difference.
- Hire and promote people with positive attitudes to customer service as well as technical skills.
- Reward good service: link team performance in terms of customer service to pay and other financial rewards, such as bonuses or vouchers.
- Reward people for innovation and be prepared to accept that some calculated risks will not pay off.
- Measure service quality. Financial results can tell you a lot about your company, but they only give you part of the picture and may not be a very good guide to your market and customer reputation. Talking to customers and measuring their loyalty and satisfaction will help you improve your understanding of the service they want. Allow the team time to reflect on what's gone on, and get ready to change both mindsets and behaviour.

---

To sum up then, improving customer service might seem to cause you more trouble in the short term, but in the medium and long term it's crucial to success. If you don't please your customers, you'll quickly stop pleasing your colleagues and shareholders. Increasingly, customer service is the battleground on which companies must struggle for survival and supremacy.

# 10 Dealing with difficult situations

**Could this be you?** Who was it who said it never rains but it pours? This was always going to be the week from hell: I've got to tell a loyal colleague that there's no place for him after the latest reorganization, and another that I won't be able to support his application for a secondment after all. And now, there's this bombshell in the local rag. What on earth was a stack of current personnel files doing sitting in a skip in Station Road anyway? My phone's been ringing since 8 am with constant questions – not just from journalists and personnel, but from head office too. Now I've just left it off the hook. It seems pointless trying to fend people off, let alone make time to find out what when wrong. And as for planning my schedule, forget it!

Even the best-prepared managers find themselves in awkward situations from time to time. Efficiency is no protection: on the contrary, a reputation for competence is likely to mean that yours is the desk on which the really testing problems land.

Such problems vary in scope. There may be a major crisis that could threaten the very survival of a business, for instance the imminent loss of a key customer, savagely critical press comment on your services or a big hole in your accounts. But smaller-scale acute crises can be equally difficult to handle. One of your people may require urgent counselling on a personal or business-related matter, for example; or you may have to break the news to someone whose services are no longer required.

Crisis management and counselling must therefore be added to the portfolio of necessary management skills. This chapter offers some guidance on how to handle difficult situations more effectively.

## Principles of crisis management

A certain type of manager thrives on crisis. Some people pride themselves on their fire-fighting ability (though such people tend to be accomplished fire-raisers as well!).

Certainly some quite distinguished careers have been built on the ability to perform well under fire, and any successful manager must have a fairly robust and optimistic approach to solving serious problems. However, most people find the management of crisis stressful unless they have well-organized and rehearsed routines to fall back on.

You cannot prevent crises occurring. You should, however, aim to stop them recurring – at least those that fall into the bullet-in-the-foot, self-generated category. The trick is not to abandon crisis management and start celebrating success as soon as the immediate problem recedes. You need to analyse the causes of a crisis rigorously until you are certain that any useful lessons have been learnt and steps taken to reduce the likelihood of such a crisis recurring.

## The need for openness

A second general principle of crisis management concerns openness. In a traditional hierarchical structure the tendency is to try and confine knowledge of a serious crisis to as few people as possible. The rationale for this is that only experienced managers are equipped to deal with seriously bad news, and that others would be demotivated or panic.

There may indeed be a case for sharing a serious problem only with those who might be expected to help solve it. However, employees in modern companies are so interconnected and interdependent that the disadvantages of excluding people often outweigh the problems associated with frightening them. You may need all the help you can get, and excluding people may mean you lose cohesion and unity just when you need it most.

Major crises can stem from external factors such as economic downturn, competitors' activity, supplier difficulties or unhelpful legislation, or from internal ones such as reorganization, a defective product or serious disputes with staff. With internal difficulties the need to be open is particularly acute: a medium-sized problem can escalate into a full-blown crisis if you attempt to mislead others or conceal facts.

## Ten steps towards managing a crisis successfully

1 Don't panic!
2 Line up a trusted confidant/sounding board – you're going to need one.
3 Relegate items that have no bearing on the crisis to the back burner.

4 Imagine yourself looking down on the scene and ask yourself these questions:
- What's really happening?
- Why is it happening?
- What will happen if I don't do anything?
- How quickly do I need to act to stop the damage spreading?
- Who else is involved?
- Who's likely to become involved?
- What resources have I got – people, equipment, finance, back-up from other organizations?
- Has anything like this happened before that I can learn from?

5 Line up a special team to deal with the situation. Allocate roles and tasks, and establish authority to act.

6 Set up a communications system that will tell you exactly what's happening and gives you immediate access to the whole team. Ensure that all key players understand their role in the process and what information you need. (Remember that the leader's finger needs to be on the pulse during a crisis.)

7 Draw up a preliminary step-by-step plan of action. Prepare other contigency plans. Involve key members of the team.

8 Develop detailed plans. They should include time scales, scope for a cooling-off period, longer-term solutions and finely tuned contingency plans.

9 Continually monitor what is happening. Ensure that you are getting the information you need quickly, so that you can react rapidly but not irresponsibly.

10 Evaluate actions and reactions constantly. You'll need to modify the plan as events unfold and take swift corrective steps.

If the thinking behind your proposal was sound, and your strategy and tactics are well prepared and executed, the chances are you will succeed.

## Counselling

As the welfare of their people should be one of their primary concerns counselling skills are a crucial management tool for the 90s. In terms of scale, the problems addressed by counselling are much smaller than those involved in crisis management; but for the individuals themselves they probably seem every bit as serious.

Ethical considerations aside, the key to success in modern business lies in *achievement through people*. Recognizing how difficult it is for people to perform at their best when burdened with a serious problem (whatever its origins) most managers now accept that they may need to discuss sensitive issues relating to people's lives outside work.

There is an obvious danger here of straying beyond one's competence, and exacerbating a difficult situation by well-meaning but misjudged intervention. Professional counselling skills can only be acquired through lengthy training. However, managers must at least be willing and able to conduct preliminary conversations that will allow them to point people in the right direction when they are in trouble. Unless you have been formally trained, such conversations should not be introduced as 'counselling', but as informal discussions.

You will sometimes become aware of the need for counselling from the person concerned. Just as often, however, you or a colleague will observe signs of distress. Such signs include a sudden and unexplained drop in efficiency, an uncharacteristic failure to complete a task, or simply a general tendency to be distracted or morose.

You may be able to plan ahead for a counselling session, but you will also find yourself in situations where you'll need to draw on your counselling skills without warning in response to short-term needs.

### Guidelines for counselling sessions

- Make sure that it's an appropriate time for the person you're counselling. Stress at the outset that everything discussed will remain totally confidential.
- Listen carefully – and don't interrupt with tales of how a similar thing once happened to you. (See also page 26, 'Active listening'.)
- Show that you're listening by your body language – for instance by leaning forward and nodding occasionally. Don't sit with your arms or legs crossed.
- Ask open-ended questions to prompt the other person and try to get to the real reason for their discontent.
- Make sure you leave enough time for the other person to respond. Don't be afraid of pauses, but don't let them go on for too long!
- Show that you are sympathetic, and try to put yourself in the other person's shoes.
- Try to get the other person to come up with their own ideas for moving things forward.
- If you give advice, think about what's appropriate for that person, rather than what would be best if you were in that situation. Bear in mind the personality of the person you're counselling.
- When trying to agree ways of improving a situation, discuss the following

questions: Who needs to do what, and when? What support will the other person need, and where is he or she going to get it? If this is appropriate, when are you going to meet again to discuss progress? After any counselling session, talk about it with a colleague (not the person you've been counselling). Such discussions should cover what went well, what didn't go so well, and what you would do differently next time.

It's important to know when you should draw the line and suggest someone seeks help from a professional counsellor.

If they are available, in-house counselling services can be used as a back-up. Individuals being counselled may be resistant to this because of the stigma attached, so confidentiality is absolutely critical. It will also help if any professional counselling is done off-site, and out of work time.

## Making people redundant

Telling someone they've lost their job is probably the most difficult task any manager has to perform. You may feel that there is nothing you can do to make it any easier for the person concerned, but the manner in which such news is broken is crucial. People who have been made redundant will remember the way in which it was done for years. If it's handled well, their confidence will be less badly damaged, which may help them to find another suitable job more quickly.

When breaking the bad news, bear the following in mind:
- Don't delay – don't pass the time of day with the person before breaking the news. On the other hand, don't rush the discussion to get it over and done with.
- Be clear and direct.
- Repeat the bad news, if necessary. Allow time for it to sink in.
- Explain the reasons behind decision. Be honest, but as tactful as you can.
- Place the decision in context, for example in terms of the overall company direction or the state of the market.
- Offer support, but do not raise false hopes.

A number of practical issues must also be covered:
- State exactly when the redundancy takes effect.
- Be very clear about what the person is entitled to. Discuss any financial arrangements and redundancy packages, and if appropriate, what the process is for returning company cars or other hardware. There may be an option to buy such items from the company, and this sometimes helps ease the blow.

- Set up a date for going through the bureaucratic processes – pension transfers, P45s, etc.

## Outplacement

Any advice about finding another job should be covered towards the end of the interview – but only if someone seems able to take it in. Otherwise bring the subject up in a second interview, recommending specific agencies if possible. If there is an outplacement service within your organization, or if your organization is prepared to pay for an external agency, make it clear that these options are available.

## After the meeting

A person who's just been made redundant will probably dread facing his or her colleagues, so, if possible, make sure they don't have to walk through a crowded room immediately after the interview. They may need some time alone to gather their thoughts.

In addition, try to be sensitive when making arrangements for people to clear their desks and say goodbye to colleagues. Ask them how they would like these arrangements to be handled.

---

Difficult situations, then, are inevitable, however well your business is run. And though not everyone thinks it's a curse to live in 'interesting' times, even the most gung-ho can do with help in a crisis.

So being as open as you can is usually a good first step. And when problems are very delicate or seem intractable, having in place some broad strategies and guidelines, such as those suggested above, should help you keep your head and set about finding a solution – or at least a way of minimizing the damage and pain.

---

# 11
## Communicating clearly

**Could this be you?** What's the matter with these people? I told everyone I was going to bring out a new performance manual, and put out an announcement the day it was ready, and another the day it went live. But here are six different well-documented instances of people stubbornly continuing to do things the old way.

It's caused chaos. Customers are confused, and there were furious rows in the team meeting this morning. And guess who gets the blame?

Why can't they take the trouble to read the stuff I put out? It's all clear enough, written in black and white, in plain English. What do they expect me to do? As far as I'm concerned, I've done my job and put my message across. It's up to them to take it from there.

The ability to communicate clearly is crucial to good management. However, communications between managers and members of their teams are often flawed and can even break down altogether – not surprising considering the many potential difficulties and distractions involved.

However, in theory at least, there's no great complexity to the solution. Of course, there are technical skills involved – writing and presenting effectively, handling meetings skilfully, listening actively and so on – but successful communication starts with the acceptance of a simple principle: *the communicator has total responsibility for getting a message across.*

This chapter looks at some of the ways of applying this principle effectively in different situations.

## Guidelines for effective communication

Whether you're talking to one person or a group, remember your audiences won't necessarily be receptive. They don't have to listen to you or accept what you're saying. This may sometimes be frustrating, but it's something that you must accept if you are to succeed. Although both you and your audience may make mistakes, it's the communicator who has both the incentive and the responsibility to get their message or information across clearly.

Here are some guidelines for communicating with others in your team:

## MAKE IT RELEVANT

Ask yourself:    Is what I'm saying relevant today, or is it really just yesterday's message?

Might it even be too far ahead of its time – too radical for people to accept immediately or all at once?

Is it really necessary?

Is it just a bee in my bonnet?

*Why* am I saying what I'm saying, in the way that I'm saying it, today?

## CHOOSE THE MOST APPROPRIATE WAY OF PRESENTING INFORMATION

The way you present information is as important as what you have to say. Different situations and objectives require different approaches (see 'Team meetings', 'Individual briefings' and 'E-mail', dealt with later in this chapter).

Ask yourself if the medium you've chosen is really appropriate. Are you just being lazy or complacent, doing things the way you've always done them? Should you be looking at different media, such as e-mail or newsletters? What you can learn from other communicators? Are you using the best tools for the job, or merely those that are expedient – what happened to be available, given, for example, that you didn't plan a presentation early enough to know what you really needed?

Nothing beats old-fashioned face-to-face communication, so whenever possible, talk to your team rather than writing to them. Talking is a more human and sensitive way of getting a message across, helping you to strike up a rapport with your people, and making them feel:

- you know who they are
- they are important enough for you want to spend time talking to them
- their opinion matters

It will also allow you to get feedback instantly, and to adjust or change your message according to the reaction you receive (see page 89, 'Listen!').

If you are going to talk to a group, ask yourself how big it should be, and how it should be composed. Would some things be best discussed in mixed-function subsections of the whole team, and others in smaller groups who speak the same language and share the same experiences and problems? And what about creative tension? How important is it to have people with different perspectives (see chapter 6, page 48, 'Creating an effective team')?

## CHOOSE THE RIGHT TIME AND PLACE

We all function better at some times of the day than at others. For example, two out of three people are at their best intellectually in the morning. The post-lunch dip (2–4 p.m.) is probably the worst time to schedule an important communication. Most people also find it easier to remember what they have learnt in the place where they originally learnt it.

## KEEP YOUR AUDIENCE IN MIND

When dealing with other people, it's important not to rush into a discussion without planning your approach. It is worth spending time trying to anticipate the impact of what you are going to say on other people, and, where necessary, tailoring your message accordingly. Knowing your team is vital for this. Remember that people tend to reject what they don't want to hear, and try to be aware of how information might be misinterpreted as a result of prejudices or the influence of colleagues.

## KEEP IT SIMPLE

You should always try to use plain, direct language. This sounds obvious, but jargon, unnecessarily long words and complex sentences can easily creep into your language if you don't police it. Such language obscures meaning and makes it hard for people to concentrate. So don't say 'the proactive measures that need to be implemented in the context of the situation *vis à vis* the market as it currently stands' when you mean 'what we should do now'.

## KEEP REINFORCING THE MESSAGE

You may need to repeat your message several times in a number of ways, re-emphasizing important points, to get the full message across clearly. Some communications, such as legal agreements and contracts, will have to be in writing, but whenever possible you should back up written communications with the spoken word. Conversely, it might well be a good idea to back up an oral briefing in writing.

### KEEP CHECKING THAT YOU'VE BEEN UNDERSTOOD

Requesting feedback enables you to check that there aren't any misunderstandings, and that people have got the whole message, not just part of it.

### LISTEN!

However, it's vital to remember that good communication is a two-way process. You must encourage and listen carefully to the contributions of others, and be prepared to modify your message/position if appropriate.

### KEEP TO YOUR WORD

Communications have to be credible to be effective so you must do what you say you are going to do! If you do break a promise, your people will make you work twice as hard in future before they will believe you.

### KEEP IN TOUCH

If you keep in touch with your team informally on a day-to-day basis you'll be amazed at how much vital information you can pick up, how many problems you can pre-empt and how much better your people will feel about their role.

## Team meetings

Meetings are a major aspect of managers' working lives, taking up as much as 40 per cent of each working day.

Research shows that those who run meetings well are perceived to be better managers by both superiors and peers; those who fail to run or contribute to meetings effectively are considered to lack vital skills (which in turn affects their promotion prospects).

It's also known that two out of every three meetings fail to meet their goals, and over 50 per cent of the time spent in meetings is wasted. This can be due to:

- a lack of clear objectives or purpose
- disorganized planning
- ineffective procedures/lack of control
- a lack of conclusions or follow-up

## Why call a meeting?

It is essential that the reason for holding a meeting is clearly established. If a meeting isn't the most effective method of communication, don't call one.

Team meetings are particularly appropriate for delivering a core brief relating to the organization as a whole, and to communicate information relevant to a whole department or team. They can help people to process information and determine what it means to them both as individuals and as team members. They can also help generate feedback and ideas, and create consensus.

Legitimate reasons for calling a meeting include:
- to reach a decision or decide on a policy plan of action as a team
- to help someone else to make a decision
- to inform
- to obtain or pool information
- to solve a problem
- to air a grievance (or grievances)
- to discuss new ideas or to create them

Always ask yourself beforehand:
- What do I want this meeting to achieve?
- What would happen if we didn't call this meeting?
- When this meeting is over, how will we know it was successful?

The answers should help you establish whether or not a meeting is really necessary, clarify objectives and highlight the criteria by which you'll know whether or not a meeting has been successful.

## Holding effective meetings

Meetings that make a difference don't just happen by themselves. You must make sure that they:
- have clear objectives that are realistic, focused and measurable
- are introduced with positive language, such as 'develop', 'decide' or 'recommend', rather than vague alternatives such as 'discuss' or 'explore'
- have an effective facilitator (usually you in your role as team leader. See page 63, 'Facilitation')
- are held in a suitable place (in terms of size, resources, possible disturbances, etc.)
- start and end on time
- follow a written agenda and stay on track
- decide action to be taken and agree follow-up procedures

## Individual briefings

Individual briefings may be appropriate to explain local initiatives and developments, and to fill people in about forthcoming events. They also provide an opportunity for people to air their concerns, make suggestions and ask questions.

The main advantages of individual briefings are that they:
- can be tailored to individual needs
- have immediate impact and benefit, ensuring a quick response to rapid change
- are genuinely two-way
- can dispel misunderstandings
- can increase the commitment of members of your team

Potential disadvantages of individual briefings are that they:
- can result in an overemphasis on local or trivial issues
- are time-consuming
- may lead to inconsistency if there is favouritism or personality conflict

## E-mail

Electronic mail is a particularly appropriate medium when you need to communicate news and information quickly, consistently and simultaneously to large numbers of people. It may be a good way of delivering an introductory briefing on a new initiative or programme.

The main advantages of e-mail are that it:
- is fast
- allows you easily to reach people all over the world, including people on the move
- permits almost instantaneous feedback

The main disadvantage is that, despite its potential for interactivity, e-mail is an impersonal medium. It cannot replace face-to-face communication, and should never be used in sensitive areas such as performance appraisals or salary increases.

To make it work:
- Everyone needs access to a computer.
- People must be well trained in how to use the system.
- Discipline needs to be exercised to avoid overloading the system.

## Communication checklist

Whichever medium you use, work through the following checklist before communicating with your team:

**Who**: Who will be receiving this communication?

**What**: What information is to be communicated?

**Why**: Why is it necessary to communicate this information? What do I want to achieve?

**Where**: Where will this communication take place? Or where does it need to be sent?

**When**: Is there a deadline for sending or receiving this communication?

**How**: By what method should this information be communicated?

---

Good communicators, then, use plain and direct language, but also adapt the message to the audience. If everyone has specialist knowledge in a particular area, for example, your delivery style will probably be different to that you'd use when talking to people from different backgrounds.

The medium you use is also important. A brief memo might be welcomed as an economical way of getting something across, or it might be taken as a sign that you've got no time for, or interest in, what your colleagues think.

It may all sound like a minefield, and to some extent it is. Words are inherently ambiguous, and no one gets their message across clearly and sensitively all the time. But being aware of the pitfalls and bearing some common-sense guidelines in mind should help you keep damaging misunderstandings to a minimum.

# 12

## Picking the right people

**Could this be you?** Well, I really do think I might have expected better. There were plenty of other good candidates and no one can say we didn't give him a fair crack of the whip.

He had a lot of the information he needed in the brochure we sent him before the interview – that alone should have given him a good indication of the way we do things around here. So it hardly seemed necessary to ask him what he was looking for during the interview. And I really liked him. He reminded me of how I was at his age. I felt I hardly needed to ask any questions because I knew what he was going to say. I felt instinctively he was our type of person.

I don't see what else I could have done. I'd have bet good money he'd have been a success here. And now look what's happened. Gone within a month, and now we've got to go through the whole tedious, time-wasting business again.

Effective managers begin the task of people management at the beginning. They insist on choosing the people they are to manage, introducing them to the organization, and taking responsibility for their development in both the short and the long term.

This chapter explores approaches to selecting the members of your team, making them feel welcome, and encouraging them to grow and change.

## Interviews

There's much evidence to suggest that interviews are an unreliable means of selecting the right person for a job, and some organizations are experimenting with alternative methods such as assessment centres (see page 96). However, interviews are still the most common method of selection, so you should be aware of their pitfalls and of ways of improving your interviewing technique.

Interviewing probably survives partly because of custom and because interviews are cheap and easy to arrange. In addition, most of us believe that we can judge character and predict how people will behave from face-to-face meetings. And, of course, at some point you need to meet someone in the flesh if you are going to work with them.

During a good interview a climate of trust and openness will develop, in which both the job and the applicant's suitability for the job can be freely discussed. On the basis of that discussion the interviewer can form a personal judgement about whether the applicant is suitable and will fit into the team.

An interview also provides a good opportunity to assess how enthusiastic an applicant really is about a job and an opportunity for an organization to sell itself to an applicant.

However, interviews are fraught with potential problems, mainly stemming from the fact that an interviewer has to rely heavily on subjective judgement. Researchers have found, for example, that decisions tend to be made early in an interview, and that an interviewer's assessment of an applicant changes very little after the first five minutes. In fact many interviewers are biased by opinions formed on the basis of information supplied before the interview has even begun. Moreover, interviewers not surprisingly tend to favour applicants who express attitudes similar to their own. However, you should avoid cloning – if anything, the fact that someone is very like you should be a reason for *not* employing them.

Many interviewers also spend too much time on irrelevant matters and tend to miss opportunities to explore important matters in greater detail.

## How to conduct a successful interview

Interviews are best conducted one-to-one, but you should never rely on your judgement alone. The best model is a series of one-to-one meetings, with the different interviewers coming together to discuss an applicant at the end of the process.

Panel interviews only increase people's stress. You may be interested in how people respond under pressure, but you should be more interested in what they are capable of when they are at their best.

Ensure you are well briefed about the requirements of the job and of the organization as a whole, and arm yourself with as much information as you can about the applicant – from CVs, application forms, personal recommendations and written references. Ideally, you should try to speak to referees. But try to keep an open mind for the interview itself.

It might be a good idea to conduct a practice interview with a colleague, asking for feedback on your performance.

Give interviews some structure and consistency by making notes of some of the types of questions you will ask. This does not mean you should create a standard set of questions, but some examples to remind you of areas you need to cover will help. Rehearse the interview in your own mind before the applicant arrives.

Tell the applicant the areas you will cover at the outset, and say how long you think the interview will last. Stress the confidential nature of the process.

You need to concentrate on getting important information that has not already been supplied (use the job specification to make sure you cover everything) and on investigating the applicant's track record, since this is the most reliable predictor of future performance. Stick to issues that relate directly to the job as far as possible – this will reduce the likelihood of irrelevant information and personal prejudice influencing your decision.

Ask open questions (such as 'Tell me what you feel the benefits of working in this team would be for you') on a regular basis. Such questions encourage the applicant to talk more expansively.

Always listen carefully to what the applicant is saying and remember what they have said. Demonstrate your attention by using information gathered earlier in the interview to generate additional questions, for example: 'You said earlier that you enjoyed working in a team – how do you feel about working on your own?'

If you possibly can, try and create a situation in which an applicant actually performs the job or aspects of the job you are considering them for (see also the section below on assessment centres.)

Ensure you get across information about the organization and an adequate description of the advertised job.

Make notes if you feel it is appropriate, but be sure to explain why you are making them – for example to remind you of issues you want to come back to.

## Psychometric tests

These consist of a standardized set of questions or problems providing a partial assessment of such things as specific intellectual aptitudes, general intellectual ability, personality, interests or knowledge. Such tests should be consistent – capable of being repeated, and unaffected by variation in the conditions and procedures of testing. Their usefulness depends on their being well designed, properly administered and correctly interpreted.

Don't depend on psychometric tests exclusively – any final decision should always be made in the light of other relevant information.

## Assessment centres

These involve the assessment of more than one individual at a time by several assessors (usually people who have been specifically trained). They examine various capabilities and characteristics that affect performance, for example decision making, ability to deal with others and motivation.

They may include psychometric tests, job simulations including group discussions, in-tray exercises, business or management exercises, and interviews.

Judgements derived from assessment centres are generally found to be superior to any other single assessment technique, and although expensive, they are increasing in popularity.

## Introducing people to your team

New people need to be welcomed on board properly. First impressions are crucial, and new employees may never recover from the impact of the wrong sort of introduction.

Newcomers must be given a chance to meet everyone and to discuss with you exactly what you expect of them. They should, of course, be given a proper job description. It is important for new employees to achieve something quickly, so make sure guidance from experienced team members is readily provided.

However, you should also make it clear that once they have had time to settle in a little, you'd be interested to hear their suggestions about how they do their jobs better. Offering newcomers the opportunity to redesign their own jobs demonstrates your commitment to empowerment (see chapter 16, page 117) and self-development. Involving people at an early stage reduces the likelihood of stress and boredom, increases motivation, ensures people's capabilities are exploited to the full and minimizes any risk of resentment.

## The psychological contract

Newcomers are bound to have expectations of how they should be treated – for example that family commitments will be taken into account if a posting overseas is in the offing, and of how they themselves are prepared to respond. Existing team members will also have expectations of how a newcomer should behave.

It is important therefore that such expectations are openly discussed, and specifics agreed. Such agreements should be renewed regularly – otherwise expectations can become incompatible, which may well cause an individual to withdraw, and may even result in them resigning or being sacked.

## Developing people through feedback, appraisal and training

You should treat induction as the first stage in a continuing development process; you'll be learning from new team members while they learn from you.

Resist the temptation to leave people to it and turn you attention to other, more pressing problems. Even the best and most experienced staff need help in the form of feedback, appraisal, assessment of their training and development needs, career planning and coaching (see chapters 3 and 8, pages 26 and 68). Ultimately, don't wait for the person to say they're going before you address any problems.

---

Although it's certainly true that much can be done to help people develop, obviously they need to have the potential in the first place! And choosing people who will fit into your team is vital for good morale and overall performance. Much therefore depends on your ability to pick the right people.

It's common sense that the more information you can gather, the less risk there is of making a mistake. But even if you don't have the resources to apply the full array of modern selection methods, if you follow the guidelines for interviewing and induction given in this chapter, you will be able to build a team you can be proud of.

---

# 13
## The vision thing

**Could this be you?** If my people hear the word 'vision' one more time, I'm afraid there'll be a walk-out. We've had the big company presentation, and the official launch of the new organisational message. We've heard how important it is for us all to pull together to fulfil the vision. Round here, though, they see it as one more piece of useless paper.

I know a vision statement is no panacea. But it might be a way of getting people to focus on the future and look at where we want the department to go. Somehow I have to make it relevant to my team, get them to see it as a useful tool rather than a bit of idealistic waffle.

Creating a vision' conjures up images of company leaders communing around a flipchart, pens in hand, waiting for inspiration from above. And it's easy to assume that a vision is just a nebulous idea, couched in jargon, that directors will frame and everyone else will throw in the recycling bin.

However, a good vision can be a highly effective way of motivating people at all levels of an organization, and changing entrenched behaviours and attitudes.

Having a clear idea of what you want to do, and being able to describe it passionately, can really help you to achieve your goals. This chapter points out the pitfalls and explores how to make a vision work for you.

## What is vision – and why is it important?
Managers accept these days that it is not enough simply keep things ticking over – they must constantly seek out new ways of doing things, transforming an organization to meet shifts in markets and customers.

In order to help people embrace change, it is crucial that managers at every level share a common and compelling view of the future that will help them relate their personal goals, and those of their team, to those of the business as a whole. Such a 'vision' connects people with a common aspiration and gives them a common purpose.

Vision requires a leader or manager to be sensitive to changes in circumstances, and to be able to perceive how things might look in the future. For example, if you are running a company you might want to enter new international markets or transform the way that you use technology. Or as a manager you might have a vision of a much more customer-focused team.

Whatever the objective, expressing what you want to achieve and why in a way that creates a spark and a sense of purpose will help you to win people over and engage them in bringing it to life. A well-articulated vision encourages creativity and commitment, helping people to approach things from a fresh perspective with energy and new ideas.

## Bringing visions down to earth

Not so long ago, creating a vision was regarded as something of a mystical task. But although one of the most important questions is why it should excite and inspire people, other questions you need to ask are much more practical:

- What do we need to achieve and over what timescale?
- Why do we need to do it?
- What are the benefits? What's the positive impact it will have on our part of the organization?
- Will we have to develop new skills?
- Does it have practical implications in terms of staffing levels, office layout or technology?
- Will it have an impact on our internal or external customers?

So a vision is largely about defining objectives in practical terms – but also about making it sound inevitable, irresistible and worthwhile. The vision is not a project plan, but it will clearly identify what any project should deliver. Pulling together a vision requires time, a lot of imagination, openness to new and different ways of doing things, a real ability to stand back from the day-to-day, a spirit of adventure and a real desire to make things better. Of course, you don't have to do it on your own. You can involve other people with knowledge, expertise and good ideas. But it is critical that you are convinced of the validity of what you are seeking to achieve.

Often, of course, vision, direction and goals are defined at a senior level. This leaves you as a manager to implement concrete shifts in leadership, teamwork, communications and customer service. In order to achieve these shifts, you need to translate a corporate vision into a compelling local vision.

Whether it's your vision, or one that has been handed down to you, the real challenge is to bring it to life. You need to win people over to the cause and help you convert the vision into reality.

## The role of the team leader

Turning a vision into reality involves changing attitudes and behaviours at every level (see also chapter 5, page 41, 'Thriving on change'). To establish an effective strategy to make a vision work for your people, you need to ask these key questions:

- What does this vision mean for what we do and the ways we behave in our part of the organization?
- If it's a vision developed at the centre of the organization, how can we give ourselves a local sense of mission and commitment?
- What do we do today that will help us to contribute towards achieving the vision?
- What do we do today that will impede us from fulfilling the vision?
- In what ways does this vision make life difficult for us today?
- What feedback do we need to give the centre about this area?

Answering these questions is not just a one-off exercise. It requires team leaders to be prepared to commit in practical and behavioural terms to the implications of the vision.

This means getting back to the basics of what being an effective team leader is all about. It means the ability to coach, to give and receive feedback, and to delegate and empower people (see chapter 16, page 117). If, for example, the vision implies that the way forward is to be much more entrepreneurial, how can you help your people face up to the implications of effective risk-taking?

You must articulate the vision in a manner that means something to members of your team. The vision must be so persuasive and inspiring that people *want* to commit to it. You must also constantly reinforce the vision.

However, it's also vital that you involve your people in deciding how the team should implement a vision, and give them the opportunity to question, challenge and contest it. It is only through dialogue that you will be able to produce an effective action plan.

How you involve people will depend on what works best with your team. Some managers prefer to talk a vision through on a one-to-one basis; others choose to get people together for a workshop or group session. But however you decide to do it, two-way communication is essential to secure the commitment necessary to implement strategic decisions.

In addition, you will need to:

- Set challenging but realistic objectives – you must make the vision part of day-to-day life, so focus on connecting it in people's minds with achievable goals. Avoid unhelpful generalizations, such as 'Communicate more effectively'. Instead you might, for example, ban scrawled messages on scraps of paper and insist on short, specific e-mail messages.
- Make it clear you know how objectives will be achieved – for example, by explaining about the capital funding, new training or new personnel involved. Visions often fail because people can say what they want to become, but have little sense of how they're going to get there. This stage of the process may not be exciting, but the results will be!
- Identify the risks and try to anticipate problems rather than solving them as they occur.
- Establish milestones to monitor and measure your achievements. Everyone must accept these, and commit to improvements so that standards match up to the vision.
- Encourage individuals to build up their own vision, rooted in their own values, concerns, and aspirations.
- Recognize the potential for creativity in others and help them express it (e.g. through workshops and team meetings).
- Provide the support people require to operate effectively in an environment that is changing dramatically.
- Continue to motivate people, sustaining energy and enthusiasm in the face of obstacles (see also chapter 14, page 104, 'Motivating people').

## Possible problems

Here are some of the reasons why a vision may fail, together with possible solutions:

- People doubt it can be realized.
**Solution:** Keep the vision honest, realistic and simple. With the help of your team, work out an implementation plan in detail. Specify targets, responsibilities and timescales, and monitor progress against promises. If possible give examples involving another team, site or organization where a similar vision has been successfully implemented.

- It's ill-conceived or there are flaws in implementation.
**Solution:** Make sure you spend enough time in preparing your vision and implementation plan, consulting others fully.

• People see it as separate from their day-to-day work.
**Solution:** Help people to think through the practical implications of the vision for the way they do things on a day-to-day basis, and the changes they may need to make. A vision must become a reference point for every part of your work and your team members' work.

• People are only paying lip service to it.
**Solution:** You yourself must be totally committed to the vision, believe that it can be realized and inspire others with your belief. Team leaders must be prepared to lead the way by changing their own attitudes and working practices first.

• Team leaders have to resort to coercion.
**Solution:** People must be involved and given the opportunity to question the vision from the earliest possible stage.

• Enthusiasm and commitment gradually wane.
**Solution:** You must be prepared to reinforce the vision continually, using feedback and other motivating strategies (see chapter 14, page 104).

• It was seen as a solution to a problem.
**Solution:** A vision is not a project which addresses a particular problem or single specific objective. Instead it should inspire people with a shared idea about where they are going and why.

• It ignores the needs and rights of certain groups, such as customers.
**Solution:** If you discover problems such as this, be prepared to adapt the vision to ensure that it takes into account all those who will be affected.

## Gauging success
As a team leader you need to check continually that a vision is being communicated effectively. So regularly ask people in your part of the organization:
• What contribution do you make to the business?
• What's the relationship between the vision statement and what you do and how you do it?
• Who owns the vision?
• What is your boss's view of the vision?
• What difference would it make if you didn't have one?
• What benefits do you believe the vision has given the organization?
• What are you doing differently as a result of the vision?

Where a vision is working properly, people will tend to have a very low-key, realistic assessment of it. They will see it simply as a tool that provides common ground for colleagues and builds focus – a practical way of letting people know what they're there for, where they're trying to get to and why.

So, a vision can give people a sense of purpose, of being involved in a really meaningful enterprise. A stone mason, for instance, could simply see himself as a craftsman cutting stone to a particular shape and size. But inspired with a vision, he could see his job as building a cathedral.

This chapter has shown that, though the benefits can be far-reaching, vision isn't the preserve only of prophets and brilliant creative thinkers. With the right approach, you and all your people can come to feel you share a vision, and a common goal in ensuring you aren't just building cathedrals in the air.

# 14 Motivating people

**Could this be you?** This one's really got me baffled. We had a really good appraisal session last year — nearly two hours of it — and I've tried to do everything he asked for. He certainly seemed pleased enough with the extra money we found for him at Christmas, and I'm sure I'd have heard if there had been anything wrong at home.

But things have been so busy, and there's no time to sit about chatting when we're all under pressure. How was I to know he had his heart set on a move into project work? And how was I supposed to notice he'd been taking days off sick? I rely on personnel to tell me that sort of thing.

But he's good, and I don't want to lose him. And I don't want to find other people are leaving out of the blue. So how can I keep people interested, involved and enthusiastic?

**M**otivation is not only about wanting to do things, but wanting to do them well. The fuel for an individual's career, ideas and actions, motivation pushes people to give that extra 10 per cent and give it gladly.

Where there is motivation, there is productivity and good performance, and people are content. In other words, everyone wins. Motivation is crucial to the success of any department, project or plan, and arguably one of your most important areas of responsibility as a manager. Understanding the principles of motivation is central to the two most important management tasks: people management and project management.

This chapter looks at ways of assessing motivation, identifies what motivates people and explains what you can do to help improve motivation.

## Assessing motivation

A motivated worker:
- performs well and achieves results consistently

- shows energy, enthusiasm and determination to succeed
- co-operates in overcoming problems
- wants to accept responsibility
- accommodates change

In contrast, a demotivated worker:
- performs poorly or inconsistently
- seems apathetic, and is often late or absent
- exaggerates problems, disputes and grievances
- refuses to stand in for colleagues and avoids responsibility
- resists change

## What motivates people?

With motivating factors varying from individual to individual, from time to time and from one situation to another, motivation is a complex issue.

Motivators fall into two categories: *extrinsic* (for example cash, holidays, material goodies, security, working conditions, social status, career development) and *intrinsic* (for example a sense of purpose and achievement, autonomy, the feeling that you know what's going on and that you're competent at your job).

It is important for a manager to look at the balance between both types of motivators, and to understand that the reasons people give for staying in a job are not the same as those they give for wanting to leave one. People cite the intrinsic, more psychological factors when asked what they enjoy about their job; they tend to focus on extrinsic factors when asked why they left a job. It seems therefore that extrinsic factors can demotivate, but have less power to affect motivation positively.

A person's skills and abilities, needs, values, beliefs and other personal characteristics all play a part in determining how motivated they are. But certain principles of motivation seem to apply across the board. For example, we all respond to high-quality feedback and the setting of goals, and to carrots in the form of rewards and praise. Conversely, threatening the stick is generally of limited value – it may be effective in the short term, but in the longer term it creates resentment and discontent and so actually demotivates people.

### Setting appropriate goals

Behaviour is influenced by conscious goals and intentions. Research has shown a strong link between performance and the following aspects of goals:

- Difficulty: the extent to which a goal is challenging and demands effort in order to achieve it.
- Definition: how clearly specified a goal is.
- Acceptance: the extent to which a person accepts the goal as legitimate for him or her.
- Commitment: the extent to which a person is interested in attaining the goal.

Acceptance and commitment increase when a team member participates in goal setting and comes up with realistic and challenging goals. It's also important to bear in mind that good support is crucial.

## Control and competence

The feeling of being good at your job and being in control of your immediate working environment is the perfect recipe for job satisfaction and optimum work performance. Conversely, having too much to do, being stretched beyond the limits of your competence or not really understanding exactly what is expected of you are all recipes for demotivation.

Your team must believe that what they do or don't achieve is largely determined by them as individuals. The feeling that they are at the mercy of events beyond their control or an unpredictable boss is likely to encourage people to turn their attention to the 'Situations Vacant' pages.

## Communication and involvement

The only person you can motivate directly is yourself. Where other people are concerned, all you can do is create an environment in which they choose to motivate themselves. It is a crucial part of the manager's task to create this environment, and you can only do it by communicating effectively.

You can't expect anyone to work well if they are vague about what's expected of them and don't understand the organizational context, or why they're being asked to do something.

If people derive no direct financial benefit from the organization's success, the only way to get sustained effort may be to wage a continual 'hearts and minds' campaign to convince them that their work is important to the organization and that they are important to you.

This will involve you in:
- Informing: tell people *why* they have to do what they are doing. Provide them with the information they need to feel part of the big picture.
- Including: include people in things that matter, telling team members not only how and why decisions are made, but how they can play a part.

- Listening: show people that you are listening by using appropriate body language and paraphrasing and responding to what others are saying. Don't allow yourself to be distracted by such things as telephone calls while you are talking to a member of your team. (See also page 26, 'Active listening'.)
- Providing feedback: let people know the areas in which they are doing well, as well as where and how they need to improve. (See chapter 8, page 68.)
- Offering recognition: give praise and rewards when they are due (see above). Many management experts regard praise as the most effective motivator of all.
- Empowering others: give people the freedom to achieve results and make mistakes if necessary, albeit within clearly defined objectives and parameters. (See chapter 16, page 117, 'Letting go'.)

Different folks do require different strokes and it's a vital skill to be able to work out quickly and accurately what's going to be effective with a new member of your team.

### The link between effort and praise/reward

The good motivator only uses praise when it has been earned. Praising merely to create a pleasant atmosphere simply cheapens the currency. When giving praise, stress the following:
- what was good about what someone did
- why it was good
- what it says about the individual
- the impact on the team/organization

In addition, remember that rewards are much more effective if people know in advance exactly how they will benefit for good performance. Expectations and targets should be agreed by all parties (see also chapter 3, page 28, 'Performance management').

## Motivation checklist

Here is a checklist of practical steps you can take to create and sustain an environment that will motivate your team:
- Set challenging targets, but make sure they are realistic and achievable. Try to involve people in determining their own objectives. People need to feel in control.
- Make sure that your team is fully informed about decisions that will affect them and everything relevant that is going on in the company.
- Get more people involved in planning work and innovating.

- Increase individuals' responsibility by delegating more. Allocate work in such a way that everyone has a chance to take on more responsibility and gain more expertise.
- Allow people maximum scope to vary the methods, sequence and pace of their work. Remove as many controls as possible while making sure that everyone knows who is responsible for achieving defined targets or meeting standards.
- Make it clear that what people achieve or fail to achieve is up to them.
- Ensure that the relationship between effort and reward is clearly defined.
- Recognize achievements, but don't cheapen praise by dispensing it too freely.

---

If you want to know whether you're an effective motivator, the obvious thing to do is to ask your people. But in fact this is unlikely to be necessary. If you're in doubt, things are probably not going too well. Highly motivated people tend to produce results that speak for themselves.

However, if you think you've got a problem, there's no need to despair. As this chapter explained, motivation is not as nebulous a concept as it sounds. If you apply the basics of good people management – in particular setting challenging but realistic goals, involving team members as much as you can and giving reward and praise where they are due – you'll have gone a long way towards ensuring that your people really want to come into work in the morning.

# 15
## Putting stress to work

**Could this be you?** I used to be able to cope. When it was just the occasional rushed order that coincided with people being on holiday, it was different. But now we seem to be in a permanent state of crisis. My in-tray is sky high, I'm constantly interrupted and it's impossible to get even half my work done. No sooner do we get rid of one urgent project than another comes up, and quite frankly I sometimes wonder how much longer I can cope with all these early starts and late nights. Thank goodness for industrial-strength coffee – I don't know how I'd stay awake without it.

I know I need to find a way to say no to people and grab a bit of time to think and prioritize. But where do I start with all this chaos going on around me?

The pace of modern working life is relentless. New things happen more often. We travel greater distances more quickly. Messages are sent and action expected more quickly. We are bombarded with events which force us to recognize, confront and adapt to change.

We raise our targets and increase our achievements each time we manage a change successfully – and we learn valuable lessons for future challenges by understanding our mistakes.

Stress is the price to be paid for all this and an increasing workload, and anything that forces us to adapt or react to cope with a new situation, can cause it.

This chapter looks at the symptoms and causes of stress, and draws a distinction between destructive stress, which can reduce efficiency and lead to illness, and constructive pressure, which can be a vital element in generating high performance – the force that keeps you going when the going gets really tough.

## Stress and pressure

Stress results from an imbalance between the demands made on an individual and the personal resources (knowledge, attitudes, skills, personality, etc.) and external resources (coaching, social support, etc.) available to meet those demands.

Stress may be defined as the response to an inappropriate level of pressure. The level of pressure that causes stress varies from person to person – what may be stressful for one person may be a reasonable challenge for another.

The crucial thing to remember is that stress is cumulative; one relatively minor event could be the straw that breaks the camel's back.

## What causes stress?

Certain jobs are intrinsically more stressful than others, involving a combination of factors that tend to induce stress. For example, an airline pilot is responsible for other people's safety, and the pressure of this is compounded by the fact that the job involves long periods of inactivity and short bursts of activity requiring intense concentration.

However, almost any job can involve circumstances that lead to stress. Here are some of the most commonly cited causes of stress at work:
- excessive workload, with insufficient resources to meet tight deadlines
- uncertain career prospects, both in terms of promotion and job security
- rapid change
- the need for continual crisis management, caused by lack of careful planning and constantly changing priorities
- poor communications – not being involved or knowing how one is doing
- lack of recognition for work done well – either in the form of praise or financial reward
- bad company politics, with people feeling they cannot rely on the support of their colleagues
- work environments that are excessively competitive and/or time conscious
- a domineering style of management, which rules by punishment rather than praise

Just as some jobs are inherently more stressful than others, some people are inherently more prone to stress – for example those who that tend to be anxious, depressive, obsessional or excitable. Some of us just tend to take things to heart and to worry unnecessarily. In addition, there are specific aspects of the way people think, feel and act that make them more prone to stress (see below). Another factor is that people who tend to believe outcomes are controlled by forces and events external to themselves (such as chance, fate or authority figures) are more likely to suffer stress than those who believe they can control outcomes.

But even if you've got an exceptionally positive temperament, certain problems in your personal life may prove hard to cope with. Such problems include:
- financial pressures
- marital or other relationship problems
- problems with balancing the demands of home and work (see chapter 20)
- stressful events such as marriage, moving home or changing jobs

## Are you prone to suffer stress?

Some specific characteristics may make you more likely to suffer from excessive stress.

Read through the following questions and circle either (a) or (b) as appropriate.

1 Are you (a) casual about appointments, or (b) never late?
2 Are you (a) very competitive, or (b) not competitive?
3 Are you (a) a good listener, or (b) do you often interrupt?
4 Are you (a) always rushed, or (b) never rushed?
5 Can you (a) wait patiently, or (b) are you impatient?
6 Do you (a) tend to hide your feelings, or (b) usually express them?
7 Do you (a) take things one at a time, or (b) do lots of things at once?
8 Would you describe yourself as (a) hard-driving or (b) easy-going?
9 Do you (a) tend to do things slowly (e.g. walking), or (b) tend to do things quickly?
10 Do you (a) have few outside interests, or (b) have lots of outside interests?

## Scoring

For the odd-numbered questions, score two points for every (b) you have encircled.

For the even-numbered questions, score two points for every (a).

The higher your score, the more stress you are imposing on yourself. If you have a score of 16 or more, you really need to take active steps to reduce stress. Otherwise you may not be around long enough to enjoy the fruits of your striving.

A score in the 12–16 range indicates a fair degree of ambition and concern about time. You should be aware that you may be putting yourself under a lot of stress, and look out for any warning signs (see below).

A score of between 5 and 12 suggests that you are fairly relaxed in your approach to life. You may not make it to the top, but you might be enjoying your work and fulfilling yourself in other areas.

A score of 4 or less means that you are not merely laid back, you are more or less horizontal!

## Warning signs

The level of stress we experience varies from time to time. Generally speaking it isn't hard to tell if you're getting overloaded, as your body and behaviour function as a very effective early-warning system.

Stress is well known for its impact on physical health, but significant changes in feelings, psychology and behaviour are just as important. Its effects, both inside and outside work, are as far-reaching as its causes are wide.

If you're under a lot of stress you might, for example, get sudden headaches or be unable to relax or sleep properly. You might feel helpless, anxious, tired and apathetic. Or you might feel irritable and aggressive. You might be unable to concentrate, and start procrastinating. You might become impulsive and erratic, over-reacting to trivial things. You might develop a tendency to become easily confused – indulge in escapist eating or drinking.

Different people are affected by stress in different ways and to different extents. If you know how and when it affects you, you'll be able to identify your optimum level of pressure. Exceeding this is where the danger lies. Whereas pressure can be good for you, keeping you going and focusing your concentration, for example when you have to make a presentation, stress is always bad news.

The following suggestions should help you avoid or control stress. But remember that there are times when you may not be able to manage on your own. Realizing when you might need help – from colleagues, friends and partners, or even counsellors and health professionals – should be considered a strength, not a weakness.

## Dealing with stress

It's not easy to change your essential personality or escape the pressures and tensions of everyday life. And with jobs so scarce, even stressful work may be better (and less stressful!) than none at all.

But that doesn't mean there's nothing to be done about stress. Here are some steps you can take that should improve the situation:

- Set goals and priorities. There isn't time to do absolutely everything you'd like to do, so focus on the essentials, which only you can do. With the rest, delegate as much as you can, then force yourself to ignore – for the time being at least – the things that aren't going to get done.
- Concentrate on one thing at a time.
- Don't expect perfection – from yourself or from others. It will only make you feel frustrated and resentful.
- Make yourself take breaks, even when you're working to a deadline.
- Look at how you cope and work on skills that will help, such as assertiveness, communication and negotiation.
- Spend some time by yourself each day doing nothing, even if it's only for five minutes.
- Promote a healthy lifestyle by taking exercise, relaxing, laughing and doing anything you actively enjoy.

## Managing your time

Learning how to manage your time to make the most effective use of it is another effective way of reducing stress.

It's all too easy to blame others for wasting your time – causing you to miss a meeting, get home late or fail to get through the day's planned schedule. But you should concentrate on problems you should be able to do something about, such as:

- confused responsibility and authority
- lack of objectives and/or priorities
- ineffective delegation
- ineffective meetings
- getting things wrong first time round
- unnecessary telephone interruptions, drop-in visitors and impromptu chats
- attempting to do too many things at once
- personal disorganization and a cluttered desk
- indecision
- unclear communication
- not wanting to saying no
- leaving tasks unfinished

You can convince yourself that the reason everyone else isn't in a mess is because they don't have as much to do as you do, or because they get more support. But the reality is that every job has tensions and stresses, and everybody has to get to grips with them and do something about them. The chances are that your own inefficient use of your precious time is costing you dearly. That means you can do something about it! Resolve to do something positive to improve your time management now.

Without planning you'll never have the time for anything. It will initially take you time to make time, but it will be well worth it in the end.

To take control of your time you need to:

- assess what is important and what is less important
- assess what is urgent and what is less urgent
- analyse in more detail how you spend your time, identifying activities that consume time unproductively (see above) and exploring where the problems as well as solutions lie
- be ruthless, devoting your time and energy to where they will have the greatest effect
- refuse to be swamped by other people's inefficiency

The first practical step is to keep a record of your activities. Do this for a week or two, dividing the day into 15-minute sections and noting down what you did in each period – for example reading, writing, telephoning, customer service and meetings. Assess how effective each specific activity was, and write against it 'V' for valuable, 'D' for doubtful and 'U' for useless.

At the end of each week, count up the time spent on each activity and analyse the overall ratings. This should give you the information you need to spot any weaknesses in your time management. If you identify areas in which your time tends to slip away unprofitably, you can begin to try to focus more on profitable areas.

## Simple solutions to common problems

| Problem | Possible solutions |
|---------|--------------------|
| *Work piling up* | Set priorities – take into account how important the task is, how long it will take and how urgent it is. |
| | Set realistic deadlines (by adding 20 per cent to your original estimate?). |
| *Trying to do too much at once* | Set priorities. |
| | Do one thing at a time. |
| | Learn to say no. |
| | Delegate more. |

| | |
|---|---|
| *Postponing unpleasant tasks* | Set a timetable and stick to it. |
| | Try to get unpleasant tasks over with quickly – you will feel better afterwards. |
| *Insufficient time to think* | Reserve blocks of time – part of each day or week – during which you will do no paperwork, and suffer no interruptions. |
| *People constantly dropping in* | Make appointments and see that people stick to them. |
| | Reserve blocks of time when you are not to be interrupted. |
| *Constant telephone interruptions* | State firmly that you will call back when convenient. |
| | If possible, get calls intercepted. |
| *Too much time spent in conversation* | Decide in advance what you want to achieve when you meet someone. |
| | Concentrate on keeping yourself and the other person to the point – it's easy to be diverted. |
| | Learn how to end meetings quickly but not too brusquely. |
| *Flooded with incoming paper* | Divide it into *action now, action later,* and *information.* |
| | Set aside the first half hour in the day to deal with urgent correspondence. |
| | Leave a period at the end of the day for less urgent reading. |
| | Aim to clear at least 90 per cent of the paper on your desk every day. |
| | Don't arrange appointments back to back – you need to have a breathing space which you can use to catch up on paperwork. |
| | Only ask for written memos and reports when you really need to see them. |
| | Ask for summaries rather than whole reports. |

| | |
|---|---|
| *Too many letters/memos to write* | Use the telephone more. If you can, use a succinct 'yes' or 'no' or 'let's talk' on the memos you receive and return them to sender. |
| *Lost/mislaid papers* | Organize your paperwork on current projects. Clear out any trays you have daily. Set up a good filing system enabling easy retrieval. Keep a tidy desk. |
| *Too much time spent in meetings* | Review all the meetings you attend and eliminate any that are unnecessary. Set limits for the duration of meetings and keep to them. Have an agenda and stick to it. Don't talk for the sake of talking. Be prepared. |

## Reducing stress in your team

As a manager, you should also be aiming to reduce the stress of your team as a whole. You can help to do this by:

- encouraging participation
- consulting team members
- constructively resolving conflict (see page 62, 'Handling and exploiting conflict')
- respecting team members' privacy and fighting for their interests
- having an effective and well-publicized long-term strategy that addresses the underlying causes of stress

> Stress, then, seems more and more to be written into everyone's contract. Even if you're blessed with a comparatively relaxed personality, an excessive workload and the pace of change could push you to the limit.
>
> The good news, however, is that you don't have to go and live in a monastery to reduce your stress. If you follow the practical steps outlined in this chapter, you will be able, if not halcyon-like to calm the waves, at least to keep your head above water.

# 16
## Letting go

**Could this be you?** Empowerment? More like anarchy, if you ask me. I mean, what are managers for, if not to run things? And how better to run things than from the front, rolling up your sleeves and showing that you're prepared to get your hands dirty? It's just not fair on the junior people, making them responsible for all those decisions. I don't understand what the rush is, wanting to give them so much power so early in their careers. They're bound to get it wrong, and we're the ones who have to carry the can. No, it's safest to do it yourself. And if you have to go on holiday, there aren't that many decisions that can't wait until you get back.

The decline of faith in traditional autocratic management and the need for organizations to get closer to their customers are just two of the driving forces behind *empowerment.*

As layers of management disappear, power and responsibility are increasingly passed to front-line people who are in daily contact with customers. As a result, managers have more time for creative work.

However, empowerment doesn't mean abdicating all control. In an empowered organization it's even more vital that objectives and responsibilities are clearly defined by managers, and that adequate support is provided.

This chapter looks at what empowerment involves, including the critical challenge of explaining why a spread of power benefits everyone.

## What is empowerment?

Empowerment is a modern style of management that involves handing down responsibility to the people doing the core work of the organization. It expands the skills and tasks that make up a job, and gives team members and front-line workers greater control over decision making, problem solving, action planning, and goal setting, thereby liberating creativity and innovation.

## Why is it important?

The appeal of empowerment is the belief that speeding up and improving the quality of decision-making within an organization will lead to competitive advantage and thus have an impact on the bottom line.

It does this firstly by improving motivation and productivity. Empowered team members should feel responsible not just for doing jobs and for their results, but also for making the whole organization work better. They become active problem solvers who help plan how to get things done and then set about doing them. As a result they should feel that they are genuinely part of a team. Their job satisfaction should improve because they will be using their initiative and their talents and abilities to the full, and have control over how they do their jobs.

In addition, empowerment is most closely linked to improved performance in two key areas:
- customer service
- quality.

### Customer service

By giving front-line employees, who deal with the customers, the tools and authority to resolve problems or questions on the spot, organizations can cut the number of dissatisfied customers and significantly reduce the cost of handling complaints.

In an empowered workplace, when a customer rings up to complain, the person answering the phone has the authority to sort out the problem to the best of their ability. This saves managers' time and means that customers' problems are resolved more quickly and effectively.

### Quality

As quality is most efficiently controlled at the point of operation or production, an empowered workforce is an essential element of any Total Quality Management programme.

Increasingly, organizations are realizing they need to enlist the co-operation and involvement their workforces in delivering high-quality products and service more efficiently and cheaply. Empowerment helps bring this about by increasing front-line responsibility for quality and ensuring everyone is helping to get things right first time.

# Key considerations

In an organization run along traditional lines, the structures, procedures, reporting lines and standards often seem designed to limit the scope of workers to take responsibility for what they do. Structures in the Brave New World must support individual decision-making and risk-taking, reinforce innovation and reward successes.

## Trust

Bear in mind, too, that sharing power is not the same as delegating. Delegation assumes that the person who delegates tasks keeps ultimate authority and responsibility for them. Empowerment, on the other hand, passes down authority and responsibility for tasks to subordinates, while the manager retains responsibility for overall strategy.

Asking people to take on an empowered role means allowing them to be creative, adaptive and enquiring. Empowering people involves developing a culture that supports risk-taking. Individuals must feel free to make decisions and learn from their experience and mistakes.

So empowerment inevitably involves a manager in taking a leap of faith – trusting that as team members become empowered, they will take on authority and responsibility, actively participate in education and training and use the information they acquire to make decisions that benefit themselves and the organization. As a manager, if you threaten to pull rank, your people will find it difficult to act effectively.

On the other hand, you must strike the right balance between accountability and responsibility, by defining the scope of an individual's empowerment and ensuring that he or she understands it.

## Training and support

As well as demanding a radically different style of management, empowerment requires appropriate training, development and support mechanisms.

People must possess sufficient knowledge and skills to take on new responsibilities, and you need to consider the abilities, experience and confidence of each individual. Remember that people will need help getting used to the new way of doing things. Some may feel threatened rather than empowered by being offered the freedom to organize their own activities. Be sensitive to these concerns and be prepared to act as a coach or mentor to allay fears.

As a manager, you may also need support, especially if you see yourself being squeezed out of your traditional role without a new role to go to.

### Information and communication

The final consideration is information. Information is power, and for empowerment to become a reality, everyone must have easy access to information in an understandable, relevant form. Each individual needs a clear understanding of the vision and values of the organization. In addition, people need information:

- on what empowerment is, why it is necessary, the ways in which it will be achieved and supporting strategies
- on organizational, departmental and work group objectives
- on individual and group performance

## The manager's role

As a manager, you are the single most important influence on whether empowerment succeeds. Your role is to help employees develop a self-managing, accountable and responsible attitude to their work.

The primary function of the manager is not to be a problem solver, technical expert or conductor, but a facilitator – the person who fosters the organization's development by co-ordinating, by encouraging active participation and by permitting others to provide the specific leadership skills required.

Here is a résumé of what you need to do to empower people successfully:

- Have faith in people.
- Provide information.
- Improve communication, encouraging the free exchange of ideas, knowledge, data and information.
- Develop interdependence, creating an atmosphere of trust and confidence.
- Develop people's abilities, providing coaching where necessary (see page 30, 'Coaching')
- Increase people's responsibilities, while defining the scope of empowerment.
- Encourage initiative and innovation.
- Encourage risk-taking and allow errors to be made, so that employees take the credit and managers take the blame.
- Provide support and encouragement.
- Learn from your mistakes.

Even with strong management support, team members may find it hard to adjust to the process – and so may you. Remember that empowerment takes time, and you need to be patient to see the benefits. But empowerment should be good news for you. Instead of having sole responsibility for a range of tasks, you will have help, and will be free to concentrate on other, more interesting things.

## Barriers to success

Empowerment cannot work unless individual attitudes, team behaviours and organizational values all support it, and many attempts fail because they only create change at one of these levels, or are haphazardly implemented. To succeed, change must occur throughout an organization – involving commitment from top management, acceptance of structural change, a long-term perspective, trust between people and between different levels of an organization, and appropriate reward systems.

Surprisingly, empowerment requires more, rather than less, self-discipline. Many organizations increase employee input in organizational activities without providing overall direction and priorities. Empowerment cannot be at the expense of structure, direction, priorities and establishing expectations.

Another reason why empowerment fails is a lack of clarity about roles. If people don't know exactly what is their responsibility and what isn't, they won't feel empowered to act.

In addition, lack of trust and openness can lead people to believe that the working environment is governed by politics rather than a desire to promote mutual support. This generally leads to low confidence and morale, as people can't see how the concept of empowerment is helping with day-to-day setbacks in their work.

A final problem is that as for most companies empowerment requires a fundamental change in the way they operate, it can rarely happen without pain. Everyone involved needs to be ready to anticipate some upheaval, discomfort and stress along the way.

## How to tell if empowerment is working

To gauge the success of a programme of empowerment, ask yourself the following questions:
- Are there training and personal development programmes for those who are being empowered?
- Is clear information freely available to everyone?
- Is there real empowerment, rather than just delegation?
- Does the climate encourage risk-taking?
- Are trust and faith in evidence?
- Does the organizational structure help the empowerment process?

• Are there structures in place to support managers and employees?

If you can answer 'yes' to all these questions, you are on well on the way to creating an empowered workforce and seeing the benefits – for yourself and your organization – of letting go.

---

To sum up, then, it's increasingly being realized that the modern world requires a new approach to management. Customers' expectations are growing and changing ever more quickly as the market becomes ever more competitive, and it's common sense that innovation and commitment on the front line – from those who actually deal with customers – will help an organization meet those expectations. Moreover, the expectations of employees are also changing. These days people are less prepared simply to accept that the boss knows best, that they should unquestioningly carry out orders.

Redistributing power is a radical step, involving a change of attitude at all levels, and it won't happen overnight. But by clearly defining responsibilities and objectives, and providing the support and information people need to fulfil them, you should be able to start to realize the full potential of your human resources – and at the same time align your organization more closely with the needs of your customers.

# 17 Managing projects

**Could this be you?** It's all a bit daunting, really. The directors have asked me to lead a project team to develop ideas for getting ahead of the competition. We've only got three months to produce a plan, and I've got to get together people from all over the organization.

Frankly, I'm dreading it. Production and sales think the people in marketing are maniacs. The creatives in product development accuse accounts of cramping their style, while accounts dismiss the creatives as air-heads and squanderers of budgets. Personnel get everyone's backs up with their endless forms. How can I persuade people to forget their differences for a while and work towards a common goal?

I t is part of human nature to search for new challenges and new solutions, and that search is reflected in every fresh project.

Projects are the milestones of civilization. The building of the pyramids of ancient Egypt, the digging of the Channel Tunnel, the first ascent of Everest or the latest Space Shuttle mission – all human accomplishments involve project management.

On a less grandiose scale, too, good project management is crucial to success. This chapter looks at the manager's role in a project team, and introduces some solutions to common problems.

## What is a project?

Projects are about focused effort, and can be identified by a number of common characteristics:

- They have an objective that must be achieved.
- They have a beginning and an end, with a deadline for completion.
- They require the co-ordination of different people and multiple activities.
- They must be capable of being planned and controlled.

- They focus on events outside the normal stream of daily activity.
- They create change.

## Benefits of project-based working

The main benefits of project-based working are:

- Problems are solved quickly, because the right people are assembled to focus on an issue and work towards resolving it.
- There is greater flexibility, as resources are brought to bear on separate activities and then released for other tasks.
- Constant feedback is generated about the latest problems to be identified, and the progress made towards solutions.
- Expertise is spread around an organization as project team members move on to new tasks, sharing their experience in planning, organizing and implementing new ideas.

Whatever the nature of the project, good results can often only be achieved within the required time through the use of project teams. Whether the project is small or major, success will largely depend on your understanding of how such a team works, and how you cope with the pitfalls that lie ahead.

## Project teams

Here are four classic forms of project team:

**Functional project teams** involve members who are all working in their 'real' job capacity while still reporting to their functional managers.

**'Lightweight' project teams** have the same fairly loose structure as functional teams, except that a project manager oversees and co-ordinates the activity of team members. However, team members continue to report to their functional managers.

**'Heavyweight' project teams** are more formal in structure, but members are not involved in them full-time and still report to their functional managers. This sort of project team is probably the most common, and also has the most drawbacks. For example, there can be conflict between functional managers and the project manager over resources; confusion about leadership; lack of integration between functions; and lack of commitment.

**Autonomous 'tiger' teams** are made up of people who have been taken out of their usual functions and are dedicated to working on a project, reporting to a strong project manager.

In any successful project team, members should:

- want to take part

- prepare well for meetings
- share ideas and opinions
- be receptive to other viewpoints
- encourage and support each other
- reserve judgement until all arguments have been heard
- help the team determine the best solution
- accept individual responsibility for assignments

## Balancing team and functional responsibilities

One of the biggest challenges facing project managers is to integrate team members who have different functions – information technology, production, marketing, accounts and so on. Traditional barriers must be broken down. However, many project teams are constructed and behave in a way that reinforces such barriers, with the result that small groups form within an overall project team, all going their separate ways.

Each individual must be able to put on two different hats. The first relates to people's specific roles and the special knowledge and expertise they bring to the team. Each person provides their own perspective on the project, and should ensure that objectives that depend on their own function are met, and that any issues specific to their functions are raised.

The second hat relates to the working of the team as a whole – to sharing responsibility for team results and effective team processes, and examining issues from the point of view of the business as a whole, not their own areas of knowledge or expertise.

## Integrating project activities

Traditionally, different activities within a project have happened in sequence. For example, people working in information technology might create a system, and marketing would then promote it. In this model of project management, communication between two groups handling different parts of the project happens only at a single handover point. This has the advantage of ensuring the communication is clear-cut, efficient, one-off and comprehensive.

The disadvantage of this model, however, is that projects take longer to complete because activities are taking place in sequence rather than simultaneously. A slow and inflexible chain of functions means that opportunities may be missed, time lost and expensive mistakes made.

Highly competitive organizations – those who must get new products out before their rivals – instead have project teams with an integrated approach to solving problems, maintaining extensive communication between different functions. True project integration means that each function not only plays its traditional role, but actively contributes to a project, proposing ideas and investigating them at the earliest stage of development.

Projects are completed more quickly with this approach. In addition, because people with different functions are better informed about what will and won't work, a better and more creative product should emerge at the end.

The drawback is that people have to cope with uncertainty: as things are developing simultaneously, work must be approached in a fluid way.

## The role of the project leader

Although they overcome the problems associated with traditional structures (which are more rigid and potentially divisive), project teams bring their own problems and challenges, requiring a very different management style to that required for a permanent team.

A project leader will probably spend little time behind a desk. Instead he or she should be moving around talking to members of the project team and making sure decisions are being made and implemented. To help ensure the integrity of the final output, project leaders need to see to it that those who work on the subsidiary tasks in a project understand the core concept.

Project leaders have to fulfil a variety of roles:

- **Interpreter**: The project leader must be fluent in the language of each of the functions and make sure that communication is effective. In particular he or she must interpret market and customer needs for the team, gathering market data directly and maintaining close contact with the firm's marketing arm.
- **Coach**: (See chapter 3, page 26, 'Helping others to achieve').
- **Co-ordinator**: It's the project leader's job to direct and co-ordinate the various functions, working closely with them on a day-to-day basis. He or she must ensure that the work of each will integrate with and support that of others, conducting face-to-face sessions out of the office and highlighting and resolving potential conflicts as soon as possible.
- **Concept champion**: project leaders must react and respond to people's different interests while ensuring that choices are consistent with the initial concept, and that tough issues are raised and addressed appropriately.

## Common problems and solutions

If you haven't got the right team structure and processes, and the right attitudes and behaviours, your project doesn't stand a chance of success. The most important initial challenge is to get the team working well together and focused on achieving results.

The following symptoms may indicate that this isn't happening:

- Some members or parts of the team feel sidelined.
- There's a lack of interest in what other members or parts of the team are doing.
- Interaction is limited, and frustrating when it does occur.
- There's a failure to meet deadlines.
- There's a lack of honesty in people's dealings with each other, particularly in public.
- People are focusing inwards, on the team as an autonomous unit, rather than outwards, on how the team's objectives and procedures fit in with those of the organization as a whole.

This section looks at some of the causes of such problems, and suggests solutions.

### Poor communications

Insufficient or poor-quality communication between a team leader, other team members and different sections of a team result in tension, conflict and inefficiency. Such problems are exacerbated by the fact that project team-work tends to be typified by intensity and pressure, as a result of tight dead-lines and external pressure for results.

**Solution:** There should be frequent informal communication to bring underlying tensions and concerns out into the open.

Good communication between the team leader and the team is particularly important during the first month or so of a project, as what happens during this period may well determine success or failure. Each individual will have questions they want answered, such as: 'What will I be doing?' 'What are the expectations?' 'Are we being realistic?' 'Can we deliver?' It is up to you to recognize these concerns and ensure they are answered.

In addition, in a cross-functional team it's vital that there is genuine two-way dialogue between functions, not just an exchange of reports or one-way updates (which are typical of project management meetings). The communication of relevant information must not be saved for crucial moments, but begin early in the project and continue throughout.

### Jargon

In addition, project teams may tend to use jargon, which increases the sense of membership within a team, but may make those outside feel excluded and jealous.

**Solution**: While encouraging team spirit, educate the team about the possibility that their exclusivity could alienate others, and ensure that key people outside the team are involved.

## Unclear or conflicting objectives

These can create confusion and resentment, resulting in demotivation and threatening the whole project.

**Solution**: Everyone needs to have a clear understanding of what they're trying to achieve, at a general and specific level. Objectives need to relate both to the whole team and to individuals within the team. Never assume that everyone has the same objective -- ask them first and check! A project charter that concisely sets out objectives and expectations of success will help people focus on the same objectives. Everyone should be involved in creating this.

## Poor planning and foresight

People tend to dedicate insufficient time to planning, wanting to get stuck into what they see as the 'real work'. This will inevitably cause problems in the long term.

**Solution**: Draw up a contract book defining how the team will achieve its goals, the resources required and what specific results should be achieved and when. Every team member should be involved in negotiating the details of this work-plan, and sign the book as an indication of their commitment.

Critical milestones that are relevant to everyone should be identified and agreed by the whole team. In a cross-functional team, these should focus on how the activity of each function fits together with the activities of the others.

The plan should then form the basis for team meetings, as a way of measuring progress and seeing if things are on the right track. Ask:

- 'What have we achieved?'
- 'What haven't we achieved and why?'
- 'How do we need to update the plan?'

## Poor leadership

However much effort the team puts in, if the leader isn't respected and doesn't show the way, the team will quickly lose motivation and direction.

**Solution**: Project teams require a strong leader who can operate on equal terms with functional managers and encourage the team to confront and solve problems in a co-operative way. See page 126, 'The role of the project leader'.

## Lack of top management backing

Problems are bound to arise if it becomes clear that senior managers are ambivalent about a project. Even if this ambivalence doesn't actually threaten the project's continuation, it will seriously undermine the team's confidence.

**Solution**: The team leader needs to identify both the sponsors of the project (those who have instigated it) and the stakeholders (those who have a vested interest in its outcome) at an early stage and cultivate them continually (see chapter 14, page 104, 'Motivating people').

## Inadequate monitoring against budget and timescale

As most projects have tight deadlines, a small delay can be a big problem. Expenditure can also escalate unless you monitor it continually.

**Solution**: Ensure that you know at any point exactly how you are doing in terms of time and budget.

## Mismanaged expectations

Sometimes a project can achieve its objectives, but still fail in some people's eyes, because their expectations haven't been met. Perception is everything!

**Solution**: Continually check that the expectations of your team, and of those outside, are consistent and realistic (see page 102, 'Gauging success').

## Lack of customer involvement

All too often, project teams ignore the people who will use the end product. It's no good producing something that satisfies the team but doesn't satisfy customers!

**Solution**: Have a representative user as part of the project team, or a user group to act as experts and assessors.

## Inappropriate team members

It sounds obvious, but if you don't get the composition of the team right, the project can fail. There may be gaps in skills and abilities, or duplication of them, and individuals may have the wrong attitude.

**Solution**: Carry out a skills audit of what you need and what you've got (see chapter 6, page 48, 'Creating an effective team').

## New members

The arrival of new members can disrupt established relationships and ways of working.

**Solution**: Try to integrate new members quickly, assigning them an adviser from within the team and if possible involving them in some form of social activity.

### Lack of coaching, training and development

Without training and development, individual motivation and hence team cohesiveness may gradually erode.

**Solution**: create opportunities for training and personal development for team members, and provide one-to-one coaching where appropriate.

## Project leader checklist

Here's a checklist of some of the vital tasks for a project leader:

### Objectives
- setting clear objectives
- interpreting and modifying existing objectives

### Resources
- identifying needs
- negotiating for and obtaining resources

### Organization
- building roles
- building and maintaining structures
- securing sponsors and maintaining their commitment

### Team members
- encouraging a sense of ownership
- building commitment

### Communication
- establishing links between diverse groups of people
- encouraging participation and openness
- maintaining good communication with all those interested in the outcome of the project, including customers
- maintaining relations with similar projects elsewhere

### Overview
- seeing the big picture
- spotting links, difficulties and changes

## Monitoring
- keeping an eye on deadlines and budget
- moving things forward.
- confronting difficulties

Effective project management is vital in a company that wants to move forward – and companies must move forward to survive. As we have seen, it requires not only clear vision and objectives, but good communications and sensitivity in handling members of a team.

The upheaval associated with working on a new project can cause anxiety or resentment even amongst open-minded and accommodating people. But what can you do if you're faced with someone who seems anything but open-minded and accommodating? The next chapter focuses on difficult people and how to handle them.

# 18
## Dealing with difficult people

**Could this be you?** I can get on with most people, but sometimes you meet someone and think: 'This one's an awkward devil.' If they're coming to work for you, you need to watch your back. I usually make a quick pre-emptive strike to see what they're made of, and then either decide that they're worth the effort to housetrain, or help them on their way p.d.q.

Of course it's different if the awkward devil is the boss. What's the point in trying to reach an accommodation when the other person holds all the cards? Nine times out of ten, it's eyes down on the jobs pages, and just keep your nose clean till you're out.

From time to time everyone comes across people they find difficult to work with. A clash in personality or style can lead to debilitating conflict and unproductive game-playing, and put up barriers between departments.

Creating fiefdoms does nobody any good in the long run, as it starves departments of the co-operation and input that is so often vital for success. Moreover, personal battles soon become transparent to others, and colleagues will lose respect for those they perceive as being unable to manage their conflicts in a constructive manner.

Your ability to work well with other managers, as well as your team members and the person you report to – whether or not they try your patience – will improve your overall effectiveness and enhance your reputation as a manager.

This chapter looks at some of the more awkward individuals you may encounter both inside and outside your organization, and provide some tips on approaches to dealing with them.

# A positive approach

You will always have both positive and negative options when faced with a difficult person.

Taking the negative option means becoming emotionally involved and hot under the collar – becoming aggressive and/or defensive, attacking and criticizing the individual, or opting out of the relationship altogether.

The short-term benefits of this approach are a sense of self-protection, the release of letting off steam or the satisfaction of having put someone in their place. But what does it really achieve? You are left with little scope for moving the situation forward or achieving your objectives. You are stuck in a deteriorating situation – and you probably don't feel very good about yourself.

Taking the positive option means, in the first place, keeping your cool. This is sometimes easier said than done, but keep in mind that negative behaviour provides purely short-term relief. Taking the more difficult path of working through a difficult situation constructively, even when someone else isn't making it easy, will have substantial long-term benefits.

So try not to see people who cause you difficulties as enemies. Everyone has both strengths and weaknesses in terms of their personal style and capabilities, and everyone has different priorities. If you find someone difficult, try to bear in mind their strengths – what they contribute – and think about how you can manage or compensate for problems.

Differences may seem insurmountable, but often there is simply a mismatch or conflict in terms of needs. Identify what it is about someone's behaviour or actions that you find difficult. Then try to understand what they are trying to achieve, and why. Ask yourself what this tells you about their needs. How can you constructively help them to meet their needs and your own?

It's also important to remember that the fact that someone disagrees with you doesn't necessarily make them difficult, so don't react defensively or aggressively to objections. Try to view them as difficulties to be overcome rather than as attempts to undermine you. Respond constructively, showing that you see the value of what has been said and are using it to improve your idea. Produce a suggestion for overcoming it – or ask for one from the other person.

Of course, some people just seem to thrive on pointing out problems and obstacles. This can be wearying, but you should still try to take a positive approach (see page 134, 'Pessimists').

Being positive will gain you respect and should help to win someone over to your side. The person will feel that you value them and take them seriously, and they will be motivated to work with you. All this will help you move things forward and achieve your objectives – and, in the end, feel good about the way you've handled a tricky situation.

## Tactics for types

People are of course a complex mixture of characteristics, but you may recognize aspects of the personalities or behaviour of some of your colleagues in the following 'problem types'. They are presented together with suggestions on how you might deal with them.

### SHIRKERS

The best approach with people who are lazy and don't do their share of the work is to use feedback and involvement. Explain that you have a problem, and how you see it, and then ask for the person's help in solving it.

### BUCK-PASSERS

Closely related to the shirker, the buck-passer tries to define his or her responsibilities as narrowly as possible in order to shift responsibility on to others. The solution here is to arm yourself with factual information from job descriptions, formal team briefings and strategy documents to define the person's area of responsibility. Make sure you get their agreement to a specific outline of their obligations. Be positive about their involvement and contribution – this will, in turn, help them to feel positive about it.

### PESSIMISTS

It can be difficult to see the positive side of people who always seem to be negative, criticizing and raising objections. But such people can help you reassess the feasibility of ideas. Try not to be defensive, and calmly acknowledge that there may be some truth in what the person says. Prepare in advance for negative responses – don't let them take you by surprise. Use them to build on your idea, or ask the person raising an objection to come up with a solution themselves, encouraging them to be constructive and develop positive actions rather than just complaining about what's gone wrong – or probably will go wrong.

### COMPETITIVE TYPES

Some people seem to feel the need constantly to prove themselves, take credit for things and generally indulge in one-upmanship. The best approach here is to accept that some people are like that, and not to allow yourself or others to get drawn into competing, which will only make them worse. But you should also try to involve competitive types in teamwork as much as possible, stressing common goals and the virtues of collaboration.

## POWER BROKERS

Power brokers are gatekeepers – people who control resources – who delight in exploiting their position. Such people can be both irksome and frustrating, but whether they're secretaries or senior managers the best approach is to acknowledge their power and argue a calm and rational case for what you need.

## The balance of power

In a conflict, it is important to understand who has most power. You should always try to be positive, but clearly different tactics are appropriate for different balances of power.

Five sources of power are common and significant:

- The power of **authority** exists whenever one individual feels that another individual has the right to influence them or make requests. Such power normally stems from a person's position or job within an organization.
- The power of **reward** occurs when one individual has the capacity or resources to reward another in some way. Rewards can be formal – for example promotion, wage increases, positive appraisals, favours or perks; or informal, for example praise or statements of gratitude.
- The power of **coercion** involves one individual operating sanctions or punishments against another. Typically such punishments include reprimands, giving someone an unpopular task or even firing them. This is a very negative source of power and should only be exercised as a last resort.
- The power that stems from **expertise** exists if one individual perceives that another has specialized information, knowledge or skills. In such a position the 'expert' will be significantly more powerful.
- Another form of power stems from the **identification** of individuals with others, or admiration and respect for them, for reasons as varied as leadership style, values or attitudes.

The following sections offer guidelines for handling difficult people in relationships involving different balances of power: relationships with your team members, your peers and those you report to.

# Handling difficult team members

In relationships with difficult members of your team you should have the advantage of at least the first three of the sources of power outlined above. However, you should never think you can rely on these alone.

Here are some general tips on how to handle awkward characters in your team:

- Avoid ambiguous messages. Decide on what you are going to say beforehand, and make sure what you say isn't misconstrued. Ask the other person to paraphrase to check you've been understood. This is important whether you're dealing with members of you team or your peers.
- Make sure feedback is constructive. Make it clear that you value everyone's contribution, and give praise and rewards as appropriate. When feedback identifies problems or shortcomings, it's particularly important to stick to the facts and cite specific examples. Try to involve the other person in deciding what should be done. (See page 68, 'Feedback'.)
- Set out your expectations, clarifying goals, anticipated results and a timeframe.
- Give people a chance to respond positively, but don't be afraid to insist if you have to.

# Handling difficult peers

When clashes occur with peers there are particular challenges. You may have the power of expertise in a particular area, but you don't have the power of authority, coercion or reward. The important thing is therefore to concentrate on building relationships.

The following tips should help you deal with other managers you find difficult:

- Make it clear that you appreciate colleagues' contributions and remember to thank them for their current and past efforts. Insincere flattery will in all probability make things worse, but if you can pay an authentic compliment, do so.
- Try to introduce your ideas as suggestions rather than rigid proposals. If possible, introduce your ideas on the back of someone else's, and make it clear that you are building on their ideas. You can create such opportunities by asking for ideas to help solve problems, taking the valuable ones and offering your own thoughts for consideration along with the worthwhile ones from everyone else.
- Try to shape a conversation without sounding dogmatic or manipulative, by using phrases such as: 'So let's recap on this...', 'To build on this, then...', 'So that prompts this question...'.

# Handling difficult bosses

The most significant relationship you have at work is likely to be the one with your boss. She or he can be your best ally and your most useful critic. And, of course, the person you report to has the powers of authority, coercion and reward.

However, there's no guarantee that they will be trustworthy, supportive or even competent. Even in a perfect world, the relationship between boss and subordinate wouldn't be free of problems.

One common source of trouble is doublespeak. See how good you are at translating the following examples – and check to see whether you use them yourself!

*Thank you for your contribution* – 'You've said enough for now, so shut up!'
*Can you shed any light on this?* – 'I want you to get me out of this mess'
*What's your workload like now?* – 'I'm going to pile this lot on you, whether you like it or not'
*We need a meeting about this* – 'I need some ideas, and fast'
*I know you'll make a good decision* – 'I don't know what I'm talking about here, so you'd better handle it'
*You're the only person who can handle this* – 'There's a disgruntled client on the telephone, and I can't be bothered to deal with him'
*I don't mean to be critical* – 'I do mean to be critical'
*This is rather a grey area* – 'I'm clueless'
*Just one tiny thing before you go* – 'Hope you don't mind missing the match/ getting a later train/cancelling your date...'

Of course, not all problems with bosses can be put down to doublespeak. Often we are our own worst enemies, because we lose the ability to articulate the one word that could prevent so much grief – 'No'!

Learning to refuse politely but convincingly when what you're being asked to do is not reasonable is a key management skill. You must recognize and defend your legitimate rights.

But you also need to make your bosses trust you, rely on you, and believe in your ability to come up with good ideas and make things happen.

Here are a few general principles that should help:

- Help your boss to be right and avoid mistakes by providing appropriate support and information.
- Respond quickly and positively to reasonable requests.
- Don't keep drawing the bosses' attention to good work you have done – if you must have instant gratification, turn to your peers.

- Don't just think about your own position – consider the whole business context. Avoid special pleading and be prepared to make concessions.
- Be positive! – offer solutions and take initiatives. Whining is depressing and unwelcome.
- Be brief – yours is only one problem a day full of problems.
- Seek advice only on problems you know you can't sort out yourself, but …
- Don't deliver nasty surprises – the kind that prompt the response: 'You should have told me about this before!' Talk about serious problems in good time, so that fire-fighting isn't the only solution.
- By the same token, you should if possible prepare the ground for decision-making by supplying details in advance, and providing alternatives and impartial advice. Try not to put bosses in a position in which they have to give an answer immediately.
- Once a definite decision has been made, it must be carried out as if it were yours. Of course you should press your view initially, but in the end you must give way even if you don't agree.

---

People and personalities play a part in every aspect of management, so being able to get the best out of all sorts is crucial to success. The key is above all to be positive – not to see 'difficult' people as enemies, but to try to put yourself in their position and look for constructive solutions. If you can do this, adapting your approach for different personalities and different balances of power, along the lines suggested above, you'll win the respect of your colleagues – and, more importantly, the co-operation of those who might otherwise only be passengers, or actively trying to thwart you.

# 19

# Solving problems and thinking creatively

**Could this be you?** If you ask me, bright ideas should be left to the egg-heads. I don't like it when Research and Development people come out here and talk to us at what they call the 'coal face'. And I certainly wouldn't want to get involved in any of that brainstorming nonsense. I don't see what's wrong with well-tried solutions. As for persistent problems, some things will never be solved, will they?

Taking the world 'problem' in its widest sense, management could be seen as a never-ending exercise in problem solving. The modern manager must not only be looking for ways of resolving difficulties, but should also be constantly thinking about change and how to develop new products and services.

This chapter looks at logical approaches to solving problems, and at ways of stimulating creative thinking.

## Solving problems

The successful problem-solver has two main attributes. Firstly, you need the appropriate knowledge or technical skill, or at least immediate and easy access to a source of such knowledge or skill. Secondly, you need the right mental attitude.

The word 'problem' has negative connotations – difficulty, anxiety, blame, trouble. People say they've got a problem when they can't see how to get from where they are to where they'd like to be. But if you can start to map out a route towards a solution, problems can quickly start to look like challenges and opportunities.

### Stages in the problem-solving process

Most problem-solving approaches involve the following stages:

## 1 IDENTIFYING THE PROBLEM

What is it you actually want to change? It's remarkable how often a group of people sit down together to solve a problem and each has a different understanding of the issue and a different outcome in mind. It is essential that all the key stakeholders agree what the nature of the problem is.

It may be, for example, that:

- There is a discrepancy between what is supposed to happen and what is actually happening.
- Planned objectives cannot easily be met.
- It's hard to cope with demands and pressures.
- People are unhappy or dissatisfied.
- Support from other people is lacking.

You then need to analyse the problem in more detail. What factors are having an impact on the problem in question? What specifically is going wrong, and by how much? How should things be? Be careful not to define the problem too narrowly or too broadly, or in terms that place inappropriate emphasis on insignificant aspects.

You should also avoid the tendency to stick rigidly to your original definition of a problem. Things change and it's important to check that the problem still exists in the form you have defined.

## 2 LOCATING THE CAUSE OF THE PROBLEM

It is important, if at all possible, to address the root cause of a problem rather than dealing with symptoms. If you don't, the problem will keep on manifesting itself in different ways.

You will probably first need to gather information. The sort of information required will depend on the problem. For instance, a systems problem will probably require a large amount of technical data, whereas an issue affecting morale could be unearthed by getting a cross-section of people around the table.

In both cases the process of identifying the root cause is the same (see also page 142, 'Cause-and-effect diagrams'):

- List all the factors which have a bearing on the problem.
- Identify the cause(s) of each.
- Identify the causes of the causes, working back until you arrive at the root cause.

A wide range of different symptoms often all boil down to one fundamental problem. The question then is whether you can actually do anything about the root cause. If you can, excellent – proceed to the next stage. If not, you will need to identify a less fundamental cause and address that. But remember, the closer that cause is to the root cause, the more positive the impact of a solution will be.

### 3 EXPLORING POSSIBLE SOLUTIONS

Identify any obvious solutions, then generate more. People often settle for a solution that comes easily and stick with it. However, it might not be the best solution – or an appropriate one at all! Use brainstorming techniques (see below) to generate a range of possibilities, and make sure you use your experience of past solutions. In addition, depending on the nature of the problem, it might also be advisable to consult an expert.

### 4 DECIDING ON THE BEST SOLUTION

You do this by:
- Identifying and agreeing the criteria for success
- Evaluating all the possible solutions against these criteria
- Picking the solution that meets the success criteria best. If there is no one best solution, integrating the most appropriate solutions into a workable strategy might be the way forward.

### 5 DOING SOMETHING ABOUT IT

You then need to plan what you are going to do and how by:
- Breaking down the strategy into steps or manageable chunks.
- Identifying what resources are needed.
- Agreeing what the objectives for each stage are.
- Deciding what needs to be done in order to achieve the objectives.
- Determining who should carry out each activity, when, how, and using what resources.

But before you start to implement the solution, think about what could go wrong, and what you would do about it if it did. You could consider trying a pilot. Rehearsing in less critical situations can teach you vital lessons and build your confidence.

### 7 LEARNING FROM THE EXPERIENCE

It is essential not only to solve problems, but also to learn from them. Ask yourself if it is possible to avoid this sort of thing happening again. And are there other areas within the organization that might be suffering from the same problem?

## Problem-solving tools and techniques

A variety of tools and techniques can be used to provide methodical ways of: describing and defining issues and problems; generating quantities of ideas and possible solutions; and reducing lists to manageable proportions by prioritizing them.

### BRAINSTORMING

Brainstorming is the most widely-used technique for making the most of a team's problem-solving potential. Its objective is to make sure potentially useful options are not overlooked.

The basic principle is to encourage the generation of ideas by deferring criticism and judgement. Brainstorming helps people overcome their inhibitions and get away from rigid patterns of thinking, and encourages the cross-fertilization of ideas.

A brainstorming session needs to be planned and executed carefully, and there must always be proper evaluation of what has been achieved. However, it's an easy technique to learn and can be applied to almost any type of problem for which new ideas are needed.

These are the main steps:

- Gather a small group of people together (up to eight).
- Explain that the objective is to encourage creative thought, and that *all* ideas are welcome. Each person should express themselves freely: self-censorship is counter-productive!
- Make it clear that no one should express any criticism or judgement of others' contributions. Opposition, attacks and disapproval only restrict the pool of opinion. Quantity is more important than quality (at this stage!).
- Define the topic.
- Call for ideas from the group. Don't worry about awkward silences – they may simply mean that furious thinking is going on.
- Record *all* ideas. Don't start to classify or consider their merits and demerits until you're convinced there are no more to be found.

### CAUSE-AND-EFFECT DIAGRAMS

Cause-and-effect diagrams are a simple tool that can help you to identify the causes of each symptom of a problem in a methodical way.

First, write down the symptom or effect you are examining on the right-hand side of a large sheet of paper.

Now work backwards. What caused this effect? Write down your answer on the left of the effect. There may be more than one answer, and it may be that the answer is merely another symptom. If so, repeat the process until you have uncovered the root cause(s) of the problem.

It may help if you use Post-it notes which can be moved on the page as new ideas come to you.

## 'SWOT' ANALYSIS

SWOT (strengths, weaknesses, opportunities, threats) analysis encourages people to look at their overall performance from a wider perspective. It involves making four lists in answer to the following questions, usually in a two-by-two matrix like this:

|  | Positive | Negative |
|---|---|---|
| **Internal** | *Strengths* <br> *What are the positive aspects of what we do, how we do it, how we are structured, who we are?* | *Weaknesses* <br> *What are the negative aspects of what we do, how we do it, how we are structured, who we are?* |
| **External** | *Opportunities* <br> *What are the positive aspects of our environment, our company, our market, our position compared to that of our competitors?* | *Threats* <br> *What are the negative aspects of our environment, our company, our market, our position compared to that of our competitors?* |

## 'FORCEFIELD' ANALYSIS

Forcefield analysis helps a team to identify what is helping it move towards a specific goal, and what is getting in the way. Strategies can then be developed to enhance the positive forces and minimize the effects of the negative ones.

The advantages of this technique are that it forces people to make a realistic assessment of how easy it will be to achieve their objectives. It also provides a balanced picture – many groups tend to focus on the negative.

However, forcefield analysis is only useful once your team has clarified where it currently stands and established where it wants to be (its vision or objective) – and, possibly, established action plans. It's also important to remember that you need to decide what will be done with the information that results – i.e. prioritize, develop or modify action plans, etc.

The main steps in a forcefield analysis are as follows:

1 Get the team (or individual) to list, on a flipchart, the factors that are hindering them from achieving their ideal state, and those that are helping them.

2 If there are too many issues to be addressed, the next step may be to prioritize the negative responses in terms of those that have the most impact (rating 1 to 3) and those that can be addressed most easily (rating 1 to 3). Issues receiving the highest joint rating will be the ones to tackle first.

3 If necessary, explore/break down issues further.

4 Plan action to address the key hindering factors and to strengthen the helping factors.

## Creativity

People often confuse creativity and innovation. Creativity is the thinking that helps generate ideas; innovation is the practical application of such ideas to meet the organization's objectives in a more effective way.

Creativity alone is never enough, since an idea is no more than the raw material for innovation. You need a systematic screening and development mechanism that converts ideas into innovations. As a manager, you must create an environment in which there is both the scope to develop new ideas and the structure to implement them (see above and chapter 17, page123).

If you want to increase your team's capacity for creative thinking, you need to:

- use the collective capacity of your team to develop new ideas by brainstorming
- exploit the variety of thinking styles different people can bring to the party (see chapter 6, page 48).
- understand the barriers to creative thinking

### Barriers to creativity

'Mindsets' are one obvious barrier to creativity. Many people, particularly if they are successful, come to believe that their particular way of seeing themselves and their jobs, organizations and problems is the right and only way. Others resist all new ideas because they have allowed themselves to become instinctively pessimistic about the possibility of change.

In addition, many people simply believe they are not creative, and so don't even try to contribute ideas. But the real key to creativity is often stating the obvious. Something that seems obvious to you may not be obvious to anyone else, and something that someone else has said before may have acquired new significance.

Here is a checklist of possible barriers to creative thinking:
- allowing the mind to be conditioned into following a dominant pattern, so that you become trapped into a fixed way of looking at things
- failing to identify and examine the assumptions you make, to ensure that they are not restricting the development of new ideas
- polarizing alternatives – reducing every decision to either/or when there may be other ways of looking at things
- thinking sequentially rather than laterally (see below) and always looking for the best idea, rather than different ideas
- not challenging obvious solutions
- automatically dismissing obvious solutions
- judging prematurely – not giving your imagination enough time to range freely over other ways of looking at things
- tending to conform and give the answer you think is expected
- fearing that you'll make a fool or yourself or appear boring, or that you'll be put down

## Developing your creativity

If you want to think more creatively, the first move is a little self-analysis. Go through the list of barriers to creativity above and ask yourself if any of them apply to you. If they do, think about the ways in which you could overcome the difficulty, concentrating on:
- identifying the dominant ideas influencing your thinking
- defining the boundaries you are operating within (e.g. experience, policies, procedures), and questioning them – is experience really a reliable guide? Do the policies need rethinking? Do I still need to follow this procedure?
- breaking free from boundaries and rigid thinking, so opening up your mind to new ideas

This will involve allowing your mind to wander over alternative – often apparently irrelevant – ways of looking at a situation. What might a competitor think of your set-up? Or someone from an entirely different field? Drawing analogies with other situations that are not obviously related may help – for example, if you're trying to get a fresh look at the balance of your team, you might look at it from the point of view of a football or hockey manager, who needs a solid defence, some reliable, unselfish, hard-working team players in midfield, but also one or two individuals who can produce the odd touch of brilliance in attack. Try to spark off ideas by exposing yourself to new influences: people, articles, books and anything else you can think of.

As with the process of brainstorming, it's vital to accept that evaluation is the enemy of creativity. List alternative approaches and postpone the search for the best one. Objections – even valid ones – must wait until you are sure you've come up with all the ideas you can. It's all too easy find plausible reasons for rejecting new ideas out of hand, such as:

- 'It didn't work last time.'
- 'It's too risky.'
- 'It's too expensive.'
- 'It may be all right in theory, but ...'
- 'The customers will never buy it.'
- 'It will create more problems than it solves.'
- 'It wasn't invented here.'

In creative thinking it is the end result that counts – you shouldn't worry too much about how you get there. It may go against the grain to delay judgement, but doing so is a vital part of the discipline of creative thinking.

The following specific techniques for fostering creative thinking are particularly useful:

## INCUBATION

New insights often occur when analytical thinking has been put on the backburner. Many of us have our best ideas when relaxing, walking the dog or having a quiet drink.

So it's important to take time off when working on analytical problems or a piece of creative writing. Alternatively, switch your attention to a completely different task.

Incubation helps in two ways: it gets the mind working unconsciously on the problem, and at the same time allows you to see a problem from a fresh angle when you turn your attention to it again.

## LATERAL THINKING

Edward de Bono's imaginative system of lateral thinking (see 'Further reading') aims to free you from habitual patterns of thought and rigid logic.

Lateral thinking is not a single technique – it involves a variety of ways of assisting the creative leap to a new 'lateral' thought. These include the deliberate and provocative challenging of preconceptions and a rejection of thinking that reduces decision making to a simple 'yes' or 'no'.

Lateral thinking involves sideways leaps of imagination, rather than a continuous progression down a logical chain or reasoning. It encourages you to apply a different perspective to a problem, rather than following the usual ruts. An advertising campaign for a German saloon car provides an example of this: the car's distinctive appeal is identified by showing the sort of person – aggressive, selfish, posturing – who *wouldn't* want to own one.

By contrast, logical thinking is a step-by-step process moving in a predictable direction. It is called 'vertical' thinking, because you go straight down a line of thought.

De Bono sums up the differences between vertical and lateral thinking as follows.

| Vertical thinking: | Lateral thinking |
| --- | --- |
| chooses | changes |
| looks for what is right | looks for what is different |
| leads directly from one thing to another | makes deliberate jumps |
| concentrates on relevance | welcomes chance intrusions |
| moves in the most likely direction | explores the least likely direction |

This chapter has looked at ways of improving both your creative and your logical thinking, and it's important to remember that neither approach is inherently superior. They are simply different, and appropriate in different circumstances. However creative you may be, you must also be capable of applying logic in order to make good decisions. Conversely, if you can't generate new ideas, it's not much help if you excel at evaluation and implementation.

So, on to the final step – although this one could be thought of as a step backwards, in the sense that its perspective is wider. Chapter 20 looks at the problem of balancing the demands of work with the rest of your life – family, friends and outside interests.

# 20 The balancing act

**Could this be you?** It's so busy round here that all I seem to do is live from moment to moment. By the time one job has finished, the next three have arrived on my desk.

Don't get me wrong – I love my work, and that's why I always want to do the best possible job every time. And when someone offers me a new project that will stretch my skills and give me a real challenge, I just can't turn it down. But as for my personal life, there hardly seems to be one any more! I'd love to go to the gym occasionally, but by the time I've finished work, there's no time. My partner has started complaining that I'm rarely around, and that when I am I'm always tired and irritable. And it's really beginning to worry me that when people ask what I've been up to recently, I can only ever talk about work.

**M**anaging is a demanding task. It's also draining. You have to give a lot of yourself – to the organization, to your own work and to your people. The danger is that there won't be enough left for yourself or for the people who are important to you in other areas of life.

What's more, social and demographic trends are making it more and more difficult to find a balance. Increasingly, both partners in couples with dependent children have jobs. In addition, the demographics of an ageing population mean that more carers will be needed in the future. All this means that in the future flexible working practices are likely to be a priority for the whole working population, not just women. Over half of women and men at work have some form of caring responsibility.

Research has also shown that though most managers look for different things from their personal lives and their jobs, 4 out of 5 said they valued their home lives at least as much as their careers. Less than 1 in 10 said they valued their work significantly more than their personal lives.

Generally speaking, people with families regard home life as the most important thing – though such people also tend to say that they get the greatest sense of achievement from work.

Perhaps the most telling statistic is that nearly half of those surveyed said that they were dissatisfied with the way they distributed their time and energy. Clearly many managers fail to master the juggling act between domestic and professional commitments.

Whatever your intentions, most of you reading this book would probably admit that work takes the lion's share of your energy. Some of you may believe that success at work can only be achieved by making sacrifices in other areas.

There are no simple solutions to the problem of finding the right balance, but this chapter offers some suggestions on ways of defining your priorities and setting about trying to make adjustments.

## Four patterns

Recognizing your current situation is a good first step. When people are asked about the relationship between their personal and professional lives, four main patterns tend to emerge. See which of them *you* recognize.

### Pattern 1

Work and home life run side by side, independently and without conflict.

### Pattern 2

Work and home life are in direct conflict. You find it impossible to reconcile the demands of the two.

### Pattern 3

Work life is totally subservient to home life, or vice versa.

You might be one of those people who work simply to get money to look after your family or pursue other interests. Your reasons for this could be purely positive, or you might be responding to disappointment in your job.

Alternatively, your career might be all that really matters to you. Again, this might be for positive reasons. Some workaholics simply love their work and can't think of a better way of spending their time.

On the other hand, workaholics may be trying to compensate for a vacuum in their personal lives, or just be overwhelmed with work. Surrounded by files and papers, some managers feel they can never take a break. At weekends they feel guilty unless they are in the office or at home with a briefcase full of papers.

These two different types of manager have been dubbed 'drudges' and 'dynamos', and there's a vast difference between being driven by obsession, stress or a feeling of emptiness (drudges) and by enthusiasm (dynamos).

However, even if you're a dynamo you should bear in mind that work-aholism can threaten your well-being and the happiness of those who care for you.

## Pattern 4

This pattern involves 'crossed wires': one area of life spills over into the other. Almost 60 per cent of managers describe the relationship between their home and working lives in this way.

Private worries or interests can interfere with how people perform at work, but it's far more common for work to spill over into people's personal lives.

For example, people can get so caught up in their work role that they can't adjust when they get home. Some managers pride themselves on their abil-ity to look as though they're listening to their loved ones, when they're act-ually re-calculating monthly sales targets.

On the other hand, some people become so dissatisfied with their jobs that they go into a decline that affects every aspect of their lives.

Any sort of emotional overspill from work is bound to affect the amount of energy you have for other things. This can make you extraordinarily bouncy or totally depressed. You might find work so tiring that when you get home all you want to do is eat and go to sleep.

Stress at work is a major source of tension in family life. Research suggests that 40 per cent of the partners of successful executives believe that stress at work has a more damaging effect on how their partner behaves at home than anything else, including travelling. Here's a typical comment: 'I don't mind the amount of work he has to do, providing he's happy. What I *do* resent is the unhappiness he brings home.'

### How's your balance?

The following exercise will help you to assess how well balanced your home and work lives are currently. Answer true of false to each statement.

1 I often go through an entire weekend without spending any time on work brought home from the office.
2 Events at work sometimes force me to miss things at home that my family have particularly asked me to be there for.
3 I often dream about work problems.

4 I have at least three significant leisure interests that have nothing to do with my work.

5 When I am ill, I tend to take work to bed with me.

6 I find it easier to talk to work colleagues than to my partner or friends.

7 It is very unusual for me to ring home to say I'm going to be back later than planned.

8 I have had to cancel at least one holiday due to pressure of work.

9 When I'm trying to read a book or magazine, I find my mind keeps wandering back to work problems.

10 I find it a relief to meet new people who have nothing whatever to do with my line of business.

### Analysis

Score your answers as follows: for statements 1, 4, 7 and 10, give yourself 2 points for each one that's true, and no points for those that are false. For statements 2, 3, 5, 6, 8 and 9, score 2 points for each one that's false, and no points those that are true.

A score of 16 or more suggests that you have a healthy balance between your professional and private life. It's not that you are not fully committed to your job, just that you recognize that the price of professional success does not have to be failure in other areas.

A score of 12–14 suggests that when work and domestic or leisure interests come into conflict, work comes first. This may or may not be a problem for you. A score of 10 or less points to workaholism. For you, life outside the office hardly counts. You may not think you have a problem, but this is a frame of mind that can damage your health and relationships.

## The importance of leisure

There are many demands on the time people spend away from work. Families are the most important one for most, but many people also have leisure interests to which they are seriously committed.

Your leisure interests can offer important clues as to how your professional and domestic lives are going. There are four different concepts of leisure:

### Leisure as recovery

This approach to leisure is a pattern that often indicates emotional overspill. It tends to involve comparatively passive forms of leisure, such as watching TV or drinking, but may also involve more active pastimes such as gardening or doing things around the house. This sort of leisure doesn't involve much in the way of conversation or relating to others.

### Leisure as relaxation
This is a more positive idea of what leisure should be, and paradoxically may well involve strenuous activity. Unlike some other professional groups, managers spend a lot of time on sports and other active hobbies, such as squash, skiing and competitive tennis. These are satisfying outlets for tension and aggression, and may reduce stress, as stressing one system helps to relax another. That's why active sport can be more relaxing than simple rest.

### Leisure as personal development
For some people, a leisure activity can be a consuming passion and a sort of alternative career. You might become deeply involved in local politics or playing in an orchestra, for example. This sort of leisure activity usually demands skills and expertise, and is more common in later life.

### Leisure as an investment in family life
Leisure activities that involve the whole family can be a real investment in family life. There's some evidence that satisfaction in a long-term relationship or marriage is linked to how much time the partners spend in joint leisure activities.

Unfortunately, however, more than half the managers interviewed in a recent study said they saw leisure as a source of conflict within the family. For a supportive partner, it's a cruel blow to find that your other half prefers to spend their few free hours without you. So an active leisure life is not an automatic recipe for a happy home life!

## Understanding what you want
Once you have established what sort of balance you currently have between work, leisure and your family life, the next stage is to work out what your priorities are. Do you want to try to devote more time and energy to your family? Are you spreading yourself too thinly, trying to excel both at work and in other areas? Should more leisure time be spent at home with the family or out on the tennis court?

It's also important to remember that priorities change over time. Check at regular intervals that you aren't pursuing yesterday's dreams, and be prepared to shift your priorities at work and in your personal life.

Here are some of the things people want out of life and work. Which apply to you?

**Leadership**: to become an influential leader; to organize and control others to achieve community or organizational goals.

**Expertise**: to become an authority on a special subject; to reach a high level of skill and accomplishment.

**Prestige**: to become well-known; to obtain recognition, awards or high social status.

**Service**: to contribute to the satisfaction of others; to be helpful to those who need it.

**Wealth**: to earn a large salary; to build up a large financial estate.

**Independence**: To have freedom of thought and action; to be your own boss.

**Affection**: to obtain and share companionship and affection through immediate family and friends.

**Security**: to achieve a secure and stable position in work and financially.

**Self-development**: to realize your full creative and innovative potential.

**Pleasure**: to enjoy life; to be happy and content; to have the good things in life.

## Developing a personal mission statement

A personal mission statement is a written statement of the kind of person you want to be, the kind of contributions and achievements you want to work towards, and the values or principles upon which these things are based. It is a set of personal standards that you will strive to meet and use to guide you through life.

Writing a mission statement forces you to think through your priorities deeply and try to align your behaviour with your beliefs. Moreover, clarifying what is essential allows you to assess what any changes in your situation may mean for you and what action you need or want to take in the face of such changes.

Bear in mind that your original statement is only a first draft. You will want to refine it as you have more time to think. And even when you are satisfied that you have expressed your innermost values and priorities, remember that you will need to review it from time to time as you and your situation change.

This sort of statement is a highly personal expression – above all, it must reflect what *you* want and are. So write it in any format you like, and cover whatever topics, ideas, values and behaviours are important to you.

Here's an example of a personal mission statement:
- Succeed at home first.
- Never compromise with honesty.
- Remember the people involved.
- Hear both sides before judging.
- Obtain the advice of others.
- Defend those who are absent.
- Be sincere yet decisive.
- Develop one new proficiency a year.
- Plan tomorrow's work today.
- Hustle while you wait.
- Maintain a positive attitude.
- Keep a sense of humour.
- Be orderly in person and in work.
- Don't fear mistakes – fear only the absence of creative, constructive and corrective responses to those mistakes.
- Facilitate the success of subordinates.
- Listen twice as much as you speak.
- Concentrate all your abilities and efforts on the task at hand, not worrying about the next job or promotion.

## Towards your ideal

Assuming that you've identified a problem, and your current situation is at odds with your priorities, how can you set about putting things right?

If you'd identified a problem at work, and defined how things should be, you would then work with an appropriate team to set out objectives for a plan of change, and hammer out a project plan with names, dates and deadlines to make it happen. We know that this process, properly applied with enthusiasm and commitment, makes all the difference.

Why, then, do most of us fail to use these techniques in our personal lives? Perhaps we're worried that they will contaminate the world of pleasure and relaxation with the pressures of the workplace.

But behind all the management jargon ('vision', 'mission', 'action plan', etc.) are real activities that get to grips with issues. They involve other people in helping you tackle a problem positively, and drive towards a solution. So, sensibly used, management techniques can also help in other important areas of your life. If you have a family and a demanding job, you won't get a chance to devote time to your favourite hobby unless you go through the process of consultation and compromise with other members of your 'team' – whether they're family and friends or colleagues.

The demands of family life need to be introduced into the working agenda. By talking about responsibilities outside work and discussing new ways of working with colleagues, you can help change the working culture. If you don't have family, you still need to make it clear that you have a life outside work, and cannot endlessly sacrifice evenings and weekends in an attempt to beat crippling deadlines.

Of course, becoming a better manager will in itself help you to strike a balance. Many of the suggestions in earlier chapters of this book – and particularly those on delegation, empowerment, and stress and time management – should help you to avoid becoming completely consumed by your work. And in general, the more effective a manager you are, the more time and energy you will have for other things that are important to you.

---

Perfection isn't attainable, of course. As soon as you achieve one part of your mission statement, another challenge will present itself, just as last year's profit level is quickly forgotten in the context of next year's targets. And no one gets the balance between home and work right all the time. Compromises and adjustments must continually be made. But if you can get closer to a healthy balance, the benefits will be substantial.

Firstly, as you won't be burning yourself out, the chances are that you'll see your job as something that enhances your life – as a source of enjoyment and healthy challenge – rather than as a burden. Management may be demanding, but it can also be extremely fulfilling. Developing your own abilities and helping others to develop theirs; successfully handling challenging projects and day-to-day difficulties; thinking creatively; working in a team; providing customers with what they want; seeing results – all of these aspects of the job can be a source of satisfaction for you not only as a manager, but also as an individual.

We hope that this book will enable you to increase that satisfaction – that it will help you and your people ensure that your jobs work for you, and not the other way round.

Good luck!

---

# Further reading

## 1 - Making the most of yourself

M. Pedler and T. Boydell, *Managing Yourself* (Fontana 1985)
Contains case studies and practical activities designed to help you manage yourself and your life, and improve your performance at work and elsewhere.

J. Nicholson, *How Do You Manage?* (BBC Books 1992)
Delves deeper into the practical and psychological challenges of managing people. Filled with activities and exercises, this book shows where the answers lie for the individual, and aids the development of self-knowledge in a managerial situation.

Michael Gelb and Tony Buzan, *Lessons from the Art of Juggling* (Auram 1995)
An approach to self-development based on the latest brain and learning research.

Mike Pedler, *A Manager's Guide to Self-Development* (McGraw-Hill 1994)
A self-development programme involving both theory and practice.

## 2 - You can't do it alone

L. J. Mullens, *Management and Organizational Behaviour*, 2nd edn (Pitman Press 1989)
Chapter 10 deals with dimensions, objectives, approaches, benefits and processes of delegation.

M. Armstrong, *How To Be an Even Better Manager*, 2nd edn (Kogan Page 1988)
Ch 17 is dedicated to the art of delegation.

R. Nelson-Jones, *Human Relationship Skills* (Holt, Rinehart & Winston 1986)
Encourages readers to accept responsibility for developing and using their relationship skills, and explains how these skills can be learnt.

Peter Honey, *Face to Face - A Practical Guide to Interactive Skills* (Gower 1988)
A useful guide to key inter-personal skills at work.

## 3 - Helping others to achieve

Alasdair White, *Managing for Performance* (Piatkus 1995)
A practical guide to performance management skills and how to apply them. Chapters look at objective planning, coaching, feedback, monitoring and communicating information.

M. Burley-Allen, *Listening - The Forgotten Skill* (Wiley & Sons 1995)
A guide to improving your listening techniques.

Roger Moores, *Managing for Performance* (The Industrial Society 1994)
Discusses the setting of targets and other aspects of performance management. Specially revized and updated for supermarket managers.

## 4 - The art of influence

Owen Hargie, Christine Saunders and David Dickson, *Social Skills in Interpersonal Communication*, 3rd edn (Routledge 1994)
A look at theory and practice of interpersonal communication, with a chapter devoted to influence.

Roger Fisher and William Ury, *Getting to Yes* (Penguin 1991)
A straightforward method for negotiating personal and professional disputes, using influence and persuasion.
D. Fontana, *Social Skills at Work* (BPS 1990)

Guidelines for the effective management of professional relationships.

## 5 - Thriving on change

Francis Gouillart and James Kelly, *Transforming the Organization* (McGraw-Hill 1995)
Guidelines for adapting, surviving and prospering in a climate of change and in practical situations, from the perspectives of both leaders and front-line managers.

D. Conner, *Managing at the Speed of Change* (Villard Books 1993)
A guide to how to make changes quickly, effectively and economically with as little political fall-out as possible.

## 6 and 7 - Teams

J. Adair, *Effective Teambuilding* (Gower 1986)
An analysis of the nature of groups at work and an explanation of how creative teams can be formed and developed. With exercises, anecdotes and case studies.

Charles Margerison and Dick McCann, *Team Management - Practical New Approaches* (Mercury Business Guides 1990)
A practical guide for managers who want to improve co-operation and commitment.

Meredith Belbin, *Team Roles at Work* (Butterworth Heinemann 1993)
Detailed explanation of the nine team roles, identified by Belbin's research, and how these can be applied to maximize team effectiveness.

Edward de Bono, *Serious Creativity* (Penguin 1985)
A review of many of de Bono's innovative thinking techniques. Emphasizes the 'logical' dimension to creative thought.

## 8 - Telling people what you think of them

P. Moon, *Appraising Your Staff* (Kogan Page 1993)
This book is intended to help line managers understand their own appraisal systems and get the best out of appraisal for themselves, their staff and their organization.

R. B. Maddux, *Effective Performance Appraisals* (Crisp 1987)
A self-instruction course, particularly on how to establish criteria for appraisal.

## 9 - Managing customer relationships

A. Brown, *Customer Care Management* (Butterworth Heinemann 1989)
Discusses the problems companies have with customer relationships and care, and gives suggestions for developing a customer care programme.

L. King-Taylor, *Quality: Sustaining Customer Service* (Century Business 1993)
How organizations can get all their employees to provide and sustain good customer service.

## 10 - Dealing with difficult situations

R. de Board, *Counselling Skills* (Gower 1983)
Examines some of the problems people at work are likely to encounter and describes ways of handling them.

R. J. Edelmann, *Interpersonal Conflict* (BPS 1993)
Looks at why conflicts at work arise and the effects they can have on our general well-being. Provides practical strategies for dealing effectively with relationships in the workplace.

## 11 - Communicating clearly

D. Martin, *How To Be a Good Communicator* (Pitman 1995)
A step-by-step approach using innovative techniques and practical examples.

## 12 - Picking the right people

S. Clemie and Dr J. Nicholson, *The Good Interview Guide* (Rosters 1989)
Shows how to prepare for an interview, giving vital *dos* and *don't*s that research has shown can mean the difference between success and failure.

G. Breakwell, *Interviewing* (BPS 1990)
Describes interviews from the point of
view of the interviewer and the applicant,
and offers examples and guidelines to
help you improve your technique.

## 13 - The vision thing

J. Quigley, *Vision* (McGraw-Hill 1993)
Systematizes the process from concept to
strategy execution.

## 14 - Motivating people

I.T. Robertson, M. Smith and D. Cooper
*Motivation* (IPM 1992)
A comprehensive introduction to the
strategies, theories and practice of
employee motivation. Recent research is
summarized and advice given on
implementation of quality programmes.

## 15 - Putting stress to work

R. R. Ross and E. Altmaier, *Intervention in
Occupational Stress* (Sage 1994)
A practical guide focusing on the
intervention strategies that can be
employed by counsellors to help
individuals suffering from stress in the
workplace.

J. Parikh, *Managing Your Self* (Basil
Blackwell 1991)
Helps managers to contribute effectively
and progressively without adversely
affecting themselves as individuals, and
so cope with stress and pressure.

D. Fontana, *Managing Stress* (BPS 1989)
Deals with both external and internal
factors.

## 16 - Letting go

P. Block, *The Empowered Manager* (Young-
Bass 1987)
Offers a path to empowerment for
managers at all levels.

M. Scott Myers, *Every Employee a Manager*
(Pfeiffer & Co 1992)
Taking the position that workers want to

excel at their jobs, this book illustrates how
companies have successfully implemented
specific concepts and practices.

Rob Brown and Margaret Brown,
*Empowered!* (Nicholas Brealey 1994)
A practical guide to the empowerment of
everyone in an organization – from the
front-line worker to the chief executive.

## 17 - Managing projects

G. Lashbrooke, *A Project Manager's
Handbook* (Kogan 1991)
Deals with the constraints on any project,
and ways around them. Also covers the
manager's daily responsibilities to his
team and higher management.

Ralph Kleim and Irwin Ludim, *The People
Side of Project Management* (Gower 1992)
How to manage relationships with clients,
sponsors and members of the project team
itself.

## 18 - Dealing with difficult people

R. Cora, *Dealing with Difficult People*
(Piatkus 1990)
An insight into human behaviour aimed
at improving communication skills and
helping to control anger and stress levels.
Also gives advice on dealing with people
of all types.

R. J. Edelmann, *Interpersonal Conflict*
(see chapter 10 entry on page 157).

## 19 - Solving problems and thinking creatively

Edward de Bono, *Serious Creativity*
(see chapter 7 and 8 entry on page 157).

## 20 - The balancing act

J. Nicholson, *How Do You Manage?*
(see chapter 1 entry on page 156)

V. McKee, *Working It Out - The Workaholic's
Survival Book* (Robson Books 1991)
An in-depth investigation by a self-
confessed workaholic.